Easy Information Sources for ESL, Adult Learners, & New Readers

Rosemarie Riechel

Neal-Schuman Publishers, Inc.

New York   London

Published by Neal-Schuman Publishers, Inc.
100 William St., Suite 2004
New York, NY 10038

Copyright © 2009 Neal-Schuman Publishers, Inc.

Printed and bound in the United States of America.

The paper used in this publication meets the minimum requirements of American National Standard for Information Sciences-Permanence of Paper for Printed Library Materials, ANSI Z39.48-1992.

Library of Congress Cataloging-in-Publication Data

Riechel, Rosemarie, 1937–
    Easy information sources for ESL, adult learners, & new readers / Rosemarie Riechel.
        p. cm.
    Includes bibliographical references and indexes.
    ISBN 978-1-55570-650-0 (alk. paper)
    1. High interest-low vocabulary books—Bibliography. 2. Libraries and new literates—United States. 3. Adult services in public libraries—United States. 4. Libraries—Special collections—Children's literature. I. Title.

Z1033.H53R535 2009
016.4286'4-dc22

                                                                    2008040028

�֍ Table of Contents �֍

Part II   Recommended Titles: An Annotated Bibliography

✖ Preface ✖

Easy Information Sources for ESL, Adult Learners, and New Readers is intended to unearth the very best from the rich lode of children's nonfiction books that reference librarians, tutors, and teachers can use with adults, especially English as a second language (ESL) and literacy students and other new readers who do not speak or read English well.

The book's primary purposes are to reveal new ways of using children's nonfiction as informational resources for adults; to provide insights into the nuances of using the reference interview to connect readers with titles at an appropriate reading level; to provide strategies for selecting, organizing, and marketing these valuable books within the library; and to identify a core list of stellar titles for use both in collection development and as a reader guidance tool.

Organization

Easy Information Sources for ESL, Adult Learners, and New Readers is divided into two primary parts. Part I, "Essential Background," contains three chapters that provide specific strategies librarians can use to better serve new readers.

Chapter 1, "Reference Service to Adults: Utilizing the Children's Nonfiction Collection," focuses on how the reference librarian can gain awareness of and familiarity with the innumerable titles suitable for adults. An overview of sources of information on children's nonfiction books, including print, online, and hands-on contact, is provided. These sources include hard copy and electronic journals

v

and Internet-accessible Web sites (e.g., Web sites of public libraries, online booksellers, children's book publishers, the children's book industry, children's authors, and blogs). Also discussed are the criteria for choosing children's nonfiction books, both series and single title volumes.

Chapter 2, "The Reference Interview: Connecting Adults to Children's Nonfiction Literature," explores the reference transaction as a process that clarifies information needs for both the user and the librarian. It explains the factors necessary to the success of the reference interview in maximizing communication with the patron and provides case studies that demonstrate the elements of a good reference interview in action. This chapter also offers guidelines for training staff in the effective use of reference interviewing techniques.

Chapter 3, "Housing and Promoting the Collection: Focusing on Children's Nonfiction," examines housing and promoting juvenile nonfiction. Whether or not adult and juvenile books should be integrated or remain separate depends on the size of the library, the perceived advantages and disadvantages, and whether the budget can accommodate one arrangement better than the other. Various promotional methods that should be considered are presented. Of course, the choices made hinge on budget allocations and on the unique circumstances of each library.

The three chapters are a prelude to the book's main section, Part II, an annotated bibliography of children's nonfiction books appropriate for adult use. Over 250 children's titles are organized into 15 popular subject areas. Many of them are "crossover" titles that do not identify children as the intended audience.

The core list of titles I selected was augmented by books recommended by public librarians (adult and children's librarians), school librarians, and children's book authors. Many contributors considered fiction titles important for improving reading skills. However, of paramount concern to them were the information needs of frustrated adult new readers who were often unable to find uncomplicated explanations of terms, concepts, and events in adult sources. Another consideration was the need of researchers and adult independent learners for brief authoritative explications of various topics.

This annotated bibliography does not pretend to be exhaustive either in its scope or its coverage. Priority was given to covering the most popular subjects and including some truly outstanding titles. My intent was that this be a "first cut" list. The ultimate objective remains for each public library to house a core collection of children's titles that is easily available to adults without requiring them to visit the children's room—a trip that would perhaps make them hesitant about using the library.

Each entry gives:

※ a complete bibliographic citation, with author, title, publisher, date of publication, and number of pages;

※ whether or not the book is part of a series;

※ a detailed annotation;

※ whether the book includes a glossary, bibliography, and/or index; and

※ a reading level.

The reading levels are intended to be a general guide. In some cases, I provide a *range* rather than a specific level so as not to pigeonhole a title that might be a perfect fit across a range of reading abilities. For example, a picture book that offers an uncomplicated definition of a scientific term or concept might have been labeled "Beginning New Readers," but because it would be an excellent resource for intermediate or even advanced new readers, I assign it a range. Conversely, for an "Intermediate" or "Advanced" title that might be suitable for a less skilled adult reader because it features an illustration program with excellent captions, I again assign a range. None of the books included would be perceived as talking down to an adult, nor would they embarrass new readers who might be sensitive about their reading competency level.

A bibliography of professional resources consulted and four indices—author, subject, title, and series—complete this work.

Only when those who work with new readers recognize the importance of juvenile nonfiction literature and the elements that make children's books a good fit for limited-proficiency adult readers seeking information on a broad array of topics can essential informational needs be properly met. Nonfiction books also appeal to some new readers more than fiction, meaning the titles recommended here can be good reading motivators.

I hope that all who read this book can find the same joy I have in connecting adults—even those with exemplary reading skills—with wonderful children's books, whether for brief explications or summary outlines or overviews of specific topical areas. The illustrations, photographs, and concise wording in these children's books are superior to what is found in many adult titles.

❊ Acknowledgments ❊

The approach to this book was practical and based largely on my own experience as a supervisor, reference librarian, and researcher. My work benefited from invaluable information supplied to me by public librarians and fellow members of the Long Island Children's Writers and Illustrators group.

I also want to thank the Queens Borough Public Library staff, especially those at the Auburndale Branch Library, as well as Peter Frost Gelber and Joyce Zucker for their suggestions and support.

Part I

❋ **Essential Background** ❋

Chapter 1

❈ Reference Service to Adults: ❈ Utilizing the Children's Nonfiction Collection

One of the great aims of the public library is to serve the information needs of the community. However, a significant segment of the population in all communities—urban, suburban, and rural—creates a dilemma for even the most astute librarian. These are adults who cannot read English well.

These individuals could be recent immigrants, poor readers, literacy students, high school equivalency students, students of English as a second language (ESL), or adults with learning disabilities. For these struggling readers, all too often a visit to the library, with or without the help of a librarian, fails to fulfill their needs. Available titles may be too detailed or may be written in language too difficult or confusing for them to comprehend. For these readers, the adult book collection may be so daunting that it frightens them away from the library permanently.

As is true for anyone, these adults need books that match their individual reading levels. They need resources that provide brief, nontechnical definitions and explications of topics and concepts that are of interest to adults, such as scientific developments and inventions, philosophical theories, historical events, biographical data, sports statistics, architectural styles, the histories of musical instruments, the origins of mass transit, and how commonplace things are made—to name just a few examples.

How, then, can the reference librarian best serve their needs? With access to broad-based collections, the librarian can play a key role in connecting these individuals to appropriate sources. Many of these sources can be found in the rich body of nonfiction titles published for children—discounting, of course, books written for the very young, which feature large print, simplistic language, and illustrations aimed at the beginning juvenile reader and would certainly insult any adult. For the librarian who does not work regularly with children's titles and is thus not aware of the myriad books that would prove excellent for use by adults, there are many resources from which to gain a familiarity and awareness of what is available and suitable.

Sources of Information on Children's Nonfiction Books

The resources that can be mined in selecting appropriate and useful children's nonfiction titles include both print and online sources, as well as hands-on contact. Below is an overview of useful resources. It is by no means exhaustive (in fact, it just touches the surface!), nor does it suggest the relative importance of any one resource. All of the resources need not be used, but any one—or in combination— may be chosen.

Reviewing Printed Publications

A broad cross section of current and recent back issues of journals and newspapers offers an up-to-date view of trends in children's nonfiction literature. They are also valuable for their book reviews, articles about the book market and the book industry overall, and lists of recommended reference and circulating titles.

Both professional journals and newspapers are rich sources of information commonly available in public libraries. Most, if not all, are also accessible online. These include the following:

ALSC (Association for Library Service to Children, American Library Association), http://ala.org/alsc

Booklist, www.booklistonline.com

The Horn Book, http://hbook.com

Kirkus Reviews, www.kirkusreviews.com

The New York Times Book Review, http://nytimes.com

Publishers Weekly, www.publishersweekly.com

School Library Journal, www.schoollibraryjournal.com

VOYA (*Voice of Youth Advocates*), http://voya.com

YALSA (Young Adult Library Services Association, American Library Association), http://ala.org/yalsa

The New York Times is the only newspaper included here, because it is probably the most widely read publication of book reviews in the industry. *The New York Times Book Review,* a weekly supplement to the Sunday edition, covers general interest adult titles but also includes reviews of new and notable children's books.

Publishers Weekly, a trade publication of the book publishing industry, covers such subject areas as bookselling, marketing, and merchandizing, and it has a book review section that spans all age groups. It provides the latest trends and news in children's publishing, features the latest children's bestsellers, and offers previews of upcoming releases. Similarly, *Kirkus Reviews* is an excellent trade journal that serves the book and literary trade, including libraries, publishers, and booksellers. It is an important source of prepublication reviews of books on a variety of topics, including books for children and young adults.

Two journals that focus on children's and young adult literature are *The Horn Book* and *School Library Journal. The Horn Book* includes articles, editorials, and other features, along with concise reviews of just about every children's and young adult book published in the United States. This semiannual journal, which is extensively indexed, is a superb resource for librarians, teachers of literacy and other disciplines, and anyone involved in children's literature.

School Library Journal reviews books appropriate for youth from preschool age to young adults. It also features articles, interviews, columns, publisher announcements, and so forth.

VOYA (*Voice of Youth Advocates*) is a bimonthly journal published by Scarecrow Press for professionals who serve young adults. Its contents include articles; editorials; columns; booklists; and reviews of fiction, science fiction, fantasy, horror, nonfiction and series nonfiction, reference, and professional books. In its reviews, *VOYA* uses a coding system to indicate the level of quality, popularity, and grade level of each book under review.

The American Library Association (ALA) is peerless in terms of the information it produces for all ages, from preschool children to adults. Its printed publication *Booklist* is a rich source of recommended-only books on a wide variety of topics, providing full coverage of award winners, editors' choices, ALA notable books, and titles on other "best" lists. The "Books for Youth" section offers bibliographies, columns, and special features that are helpful to those involved with collection development and readers' advisory work.

The Association for Library Service to Children (ALSC) and the Young Adult Library Services Association (YALSA) are divisions of the ALA and are dedicated to supporting and enhancing library service to children and young adults by supporting service to these age groups in all types of libraries.

The ALSC administers a number of awards, the most prestigious of which are the Newbery and Caldecott medals for outstanding contributions to children's literature by authors and illustrators during the preceding year. Another award of interest is the Robert F. Sibert Informational Book Award for the most distinguished informational book published during the preceding year. The ALSC also publishes lists of notable books for children.

The YALSA awards include the Alex Awards, given annually to ten books written for adults that have special appeal to young adults; the Margaret A. Edwards Award, honoring an author and the body of his or her work for their lifetime contribution of books of enduring popularity for teenagers; the Michael L. Printz Award, which honors excellence in literature written for young adults; and the new YALSA Award for Excellence in Nonfiction for Young Adults, which will honor the year's best nonfiction book for young adults. The first winner will be named in 2010. YALSA also publishes lists such as "Best Books for Young Adults," chosen from the current year's books, and "Outstanding Books for the College Bound."

Searching the Web

Not enough can be said about the power of the Internet to provide the most current and wide-ranging access to electronic resources available.

Public Libraries

Public library Web sites are easily accessible through the Internet. They provide links to library catalogs, electronic databases, and a variety of other services and Internet sites. Being able to study and share freely in what other urban, suburban, and rural libraries have done with their Web sites in terms of content and design provides excellent ideas for one's own library Web site.

Library homepages are of particular interest in terms of their content and the way the information is arranged. Many libraries are very innovative in their homepage design and provide colorful presentations, announcing upcoming special events and workshops, posting newsletters and flyers, and providing lists of new titles on specific topics and short bibliographies on subjects of interest to specific audiences—for example, ESL and literacy students. Frequent updates of the homepage keep it current.

Links to in-house and remote databases are evaluated according to their accuracy, quality, and usefulness to the library staff and patrons alike. Questions about databases under consideration for acquisition can be answered by looking at what databases are offered by other libraries. Most likely they were selected because their content is considered authoritative, accurate, and up to date; their access is consistently available and free; their design is well organized; and they are easy to search. Indeed, looking at public library Web sites is educational, a tool to be used to enhance one's own site and a perfect solution to answering queries that are regional in nature and not available otherwise.

The following is a small random sample of the many library Web sites available:

Columbus Metropolitan Library, Ohio, www.columbus
library.org

King County Library System, Washington, www.kcls.org

Los Angeles Public Library, www.lapl.org

Library of Congress, www.loc.gov

New York Public Library, http://nypl.org

Queens Borough Public Library, New York, http://queens
library.org

Online Booksellers

Locating information on books being considered for acquisition is easy and painless when the vast resources of online booksellers are mined. Their fast search engines make it possible to find appropriate books in any topical category or area of interest and for all levels of reading competency. The searcher can browse through any number of categories or search by title, author, or keyword. Full book entries offer titles, excerpts, journal and customer reviews, short biographies of authors, author blogs, and access to other booksellers for new and used copies of in-print and out-of-print titles. The sizes of different bookseller sites range from quite large to vast, as in the case of the teamed amazon.com and borders.com and its resulting mega database.

Following is a sampling of popular sites:

http://A1Books.com

www.AbeBooks.com

www.amazon.com

www.barnesandnoble.com

www.borders.com

http://powells.com

Children's Book Publishers

Children's book publisher Web sites are ideal for focusing on the nonfiction subjects handled by particular publishing houses and on the single titles and series they publish. Quick access to publishers can easily be found in various writers' guides, the most comprehensive of which is the *Children's Writers and Illustrator's Market*. Published annually by Writer's Digest Books, it is written for writers and features a comprehensive list of major publishers. Entries give contact information and the Web site address of each publisher. Of special interest is a subject index that lists publishers of nonfiction by subject for efficient identification.

The following is a brief sampling of publishers of children's nonfiction titles:

Barron's Educational Series, http://barronseduc.com

Capstone Press, www.capstonepress.com

Chelsea House, http://chelseahouse.com

DK Publishing, Inc., http://dk.com

Holiday House, Inc., http://holidayhouse.com

Houghton Mifflin Co., http://houghtonmifflinbooks.com

Lerner Publishing Group, www.lernerbooks.com

Scholastic Press, www.scholastic.com

Viking Children's Books (Penguin Group, Inc.),
    http://penguin.com

Walker Company, http://walkeryoungreaders.com

Web Sites About the Children's Book Industry

Web sites featuring book industry news, statistics, reviews, author information, publishers' lists, and more are just a click away. These comprehensive sites target a varied audience of authors, editors, illustrators, booksellers, teachers, librarians, writers, and publishers. Some sites offer free access, while others require a membership fee. Following are three examples of the many informative sites offering a variety of data.

Bowker refers to its *BookWire* Web site (http://bookwire.com) as "the book industry resource." Dedicated to presenting the latest information on the book industry, its features include themed book lists, publishers' homepages, author biographies, in-depth interviews with *BookWire* authors, book industry statistics, press releases, *BookWire*–featured titles, and the latest news of the book industry from around the world.

The Children's Literature Comprehensive Database (CLDC) offers over 315,000 full-text searchable reviews of children's books at http://childrenslit.com. This acquisition, research, and reference tool has MARC records and reviews from 37 reviewers, including *Booklist*, *The Horn Book*, and *Kirkus Reviews*. Subscribers can search by subject, age level, and genre. Also provided are teaching tools such as lesson plans and teaching guides and links to thousands of author and illustrator Web pages. This appealing site is available to subscribers at a low cost.

Jacketflap (www.jacketflap.com), described as a social networking community, is a comprehensive resource for information on the children's book industry for writers, illustrators, librarians, teachers, editors, publishers, agents, booksellers, and others. Membership is free, and members can search a large database on children's book publishers, view book-related postings from its blog readers, research publisher information, and search a member directory for authors who might be interested in visiting a library for book signings or readings. The homepage features "just released children's and YA books" and recent Jacketflap news. The site is easy to navigate and chock full of data.

Author Web Sites

If you want to locate all sorts of information about authors, their Web sites are the places to go. Authors provide personal profiles; overviews of their books, published and forthcoming; the awards they've won; their articles on writing, and more. Most provide links to their publishers. Three sample sites by nonfiction authors are described. (*Note:* All three of these authors are included in the annotated bibliography in Part II.)

Donna Hicks's Web site (www.donnahicks.com) is modest and simple to navigate. She identifies herself as a national board-certified teacher with a master's degree in education. There are links to information about her teaching and writing and about her book(s); to "stuff for teachers"; and to her husband's Web site. There is a "more links" icon that leads to a list of children's authors and illustrators; a second click takes you to another author's Web site. There is also a link to Barnes & Noble.

On Joy Hakim's more elaborate Web site (http://joyhakim.com), you can read her biography, view her books and purchase them, access information for teachers, and contact the author. The covers of her history and science series books appear on the homepage and are clickable. There are links to Smithsonian Books, Oxford University Press, Amazon, Barnes & Noble, and other publishers. A link to finding other authors is also available.

Kathleen Krull's Web site (http://kathleenkrull.com) opens to a colorful page of her books and a brief lighthearted bit of biographical information. With a click on any book written by this prolific writer, an introduction to the book pops up. You can also look at information on the "cast of characters," her reviews and awards, her activities, and her "Lives of..." series titles. In addition to her books and her biographical data, there is a link to her e-mail address.

Numerous sources have author lists and links, but the express route to locating an author's Web site is through a simple Google search.

Blogs

The term *blog* is derived from *web log*. A blog is a Web site with regular entries of commentary or news on a particular subject and usually provides links to other blogs and Web sites on related topics. Links to blogs of interest to librarians and teachers are commonly found on the Web sites of public libraries, professional journals, and other members of the book industry. A few samples include the following:

http://bunnyplanet.blogspot.com (Blog from the Windowsill)

http://clarklibrary.blogspot.com (Clark County Public
Library, Nebraska)

http://hbook.com/blog (Read Roger: *The Horn Book* Editor's Rants and Raves)

www.jacketflap.com/megablog/blogs (sponsored group)

www.loc.gov/blog (Library of Congress)

www.madisonpubliclibrary.org/services/blogs.html (Madison Public Library, Wisconsin)

www.schoollibraryjournal.com/blogs (*School Library Journal*)

http://sfpl.lib.ca.us/news/blogs (San Francisco Public Library)

Other Sources of Information

In addition to printed and online resources, much can be gained by hands-on investigation—that is, field research. This would include visiting local bookstores to browse the shelves, examine new titles, and observe how the books are displayed and which children's titles are featured. This expedition into the field can be an enjoyable experience as well as an enlightening one.

Another excellent source is the children's department at the local public library. There, too, browsing the shelves, examining new titles and their contents, and observing the book displays can provide useful ideas regarding the books—and types of books—you might want to include in your own children's and adult nonfiction collections.

Establishing an informal consulting partnership between reference department librarians and the librarians in the children's department to discuss book selection methods and titles that might be recommended for adults is an efficient way to learn about books appropriate for adults across a range of reading levels. In-house orientation and training sessions are also useful venues.

Criteria for Choosing Children's Nonfiction Books

Once you have decided to supplement your adult collection with nonfiction children's titles, you must closely examine the individual titles to determine their usefulness and appropriateness before recommending them to any adult—particularly adults who do not speak English well—and other new readers. Many children's nonfiction books are appealing to adults whether or not they are new or experienced readers because they address subjects in a straightforward manner, convey information simply and accurately, and make extensive use of appealing photographs, illustrations, and graphic materials. They are well researched and written in a style that is not condescending and does not identify children as the target audience.

It is up to the librarian, who is expert in connecting adults to the appropriate sources, to decide what will fill a patron's needs most quickly and effectively. For example, if a patron asks what happened in the aftermath of the Civil War, the librarian must do a great deal more than merely point to the shelves. Armed with solid knowledge of the adult and children's nonfiction titles available—along with information gathered during the reference interview—the librarian can make judgments about the reader's real need and reading level and guide him or her to either a two-inch tome on the Reconstruction Period or an excellent children's nonfiction title, such as Tonya Bolden's *Cause: Reconstruction America, 1863–1877* (New York: Knopf, 2005: 138 pages). This modest book offers a concise overview, clearly stated.

The number of children's nonfiction titles appropriate for adults continues to expand. Evidence of the significance of children's nonfiction books for fulfilling adult information needs can be found in bookstore displays and public library nonfiction sections where they are more and more often shelved with adult titles. To evaluate the appropriateness of juvenile books, librarians should base their judgment on a number of criteria, which, depending on the subject matter, may include the following:

- ✖ The information is presented with authority.
- ✖ The content is presented clearly and concisely.
- ✖ The writing style is clear and avoids highly technical terminology or jargon, yet it is not so simple that it insults the adult reader's intelligence.

- ✖ The book is rich with adult-oriented illustrations that enhance the text.
- ✖ The book's dimensions and print size are appealing and appropriate for adults.
- ✖ The cover and title are appealing and do not appear juvenile.
- ✖ The book has a table of contents and an index that are sufficiently detailed so that the reader can quickly assess its usefulness.
- ✖ If the book is illustrated, there are ample captions and labels that clarify the illustrations and enhance the text.
- ✖ Where appropriate, there are pedagogical elements such as fact boxes and highlighted pages that provide supplementary information.
- ✖ There is a glossary, chronology, or time line, if appropriate.
- ✖ A bibliography is included, enhancing the credibility of the contents.

Books in Series and Single Title Volumes

A vast number of children's nonfiction books are published in series intended to introduce readers to related topics in a wide variety of subjects. For the most part, each volume is series independent (i.e., self-standing) and therefore can be considered for purchase to fill a need for information on a particular aspect of a broader subject.

For example, if a patron with a moderate command of English is looking for books that trace the history of information storage and retrieval, the knowledgeable librarian might guide him or her to a brief history of the book—such as Karen Brookfield's *Book* (New York: DK, 2000: 64 pages), which is part of the Eyewitness Books series. In this attractive volume, the text and illustrations are combined to present a wealth of information in an exciting package. Moving on to the electronic age, the librarian might then guide the patron to the shelves to show him or her the choices available—for example, Josepha Sherman's *The History of the Internet* (New York: Franklin Watts, 2003: 64 pages), which is part of the Watts Library series. This modest book explores the history of the Internet from its origins to its future capabilities. Either the librarian or the patron might spy a companion volume in the same series by the same author, *The History of the Personal Computer* (New York: Franklin Watts, 2003: 64 pages). Because this book provides a concise overview of smaller electronic information and storage devices, it is perfectly fitted to the patron's needs and reading level.

If a patron with a fascination for architecture asks for books on buildings in America, the librarian must determine whether or not he or she is interested in nontechnical sources on big projects like "bridges and stuff." If so, George Sullivan's *Built to Last: Building America's Amazing Bridges, Dams, Tunnels, and Skyscrapers* (New York: Scholastic, 2005: 128 pages) would be a perfect choice. It provides an overview of the design and construction of 17 architectural and engineering wonders. In one instance, the reader's casual fascination with architecture was so obvious that the librarian selected one of her favorite nontraditional books on famous buildings that were at first despised as eyesores—Susan Goldman Rubin's *There Goes the Neighborhood: Ten Buildings People Love to Hate* (New York: Holiday House, 2001: 96 pages). The patron thumbed through it, and after reading that the Washington Monument was likened to a stalk of asparagus, he was intrigued and borrowed it.

These books—whether single titles or volumes in a series—represent a mere sampling of titles suitable for adults. The range of subjects is vast—covering everything from recipes for parrots (Robin Deutsch's *The Healthy Bird Cookbook*, Neptune City, NJ: T.F.H., 2004: 192 pages) to a dictionary of physics (Corrine Stockley, Chris Oxlade, and Jane Wertheim's *Illustrated Dictionary of Physics*, Tulsa, OK: EDC, 128 pages). Book lengths vary from picture books with concise explications of the rainforest (Jen Green's *Rainforest Revealed*) to discussions of a single aspect of the human body (Patricia Macnair's *Brain Power: The Brain, Nervous System, and Senses*, Ashmore City, Australia: Kingfisher, 2005: 40 pages) to detailed volumes notable for being clearly written, with concise entries enriched with illustrations and other features that enhance the text. These include titles on various aspects of American history (Mark H. Bockenhauer and Stephen Cunha's *Our Fifty States*, Washington, DC: National Geographic Society, 2004: 239 pages) and science (Melvin Berger's *Scholastic Science Dictionary*, New York: Scholastic, 2000: 224 pages). All of these resources are described in the annotated bibliography in Part II.

As is true in any library, selection depends on the patrons. Increasingly, research interests, reading levels, and English language competency demand that the adult book collection become more diverse in scope. Reference librarians have to gain expertise in utilizing children's nonfiction titles and have much to consider.

Summary

The most informative resources in the world are useless to an adult who cannot read at the level for which they were written. Recent immigrants, poor readers, literacy students, high school equivalency students, ESL students, and adults with learning disabilities require books that match their individual reading levels. The nonfiction children's collection offers an abundance of resources written at varying reading levels and covering a vast array of topics and subject areas.

For the librarian who wants to mine this resource but who is unfamiliar with children's nonfiction, there are numerous sources of information that can be used, from printed publications, such as newspapers and journals; to Internet searches to access the Web sites of other libraries, online booksellers, children's book publishers, authors, and bloggers; to hands-on research, including visits to bookstores and other libraries and consultations with children's librarians.

The near infinite choice of available titles could seem overwhelming, but there are criteria to consider when evaluating a book's appropriateness—such as clarity of writing; avoidance of jargon or highly technical terminology; whether or not a bibliography, glossary, and index are included; and the book's dimensions and print size.

The reference librarian who is able to competently select and evaluate children's books for adults becomes the link between the data needed and the appropriate book to satisfy that need. As in all reference transactions, the reference interview is key in determining exactly what a patron is looking for. The reference interview is discussed in Chapter 2.

Chapter 2

❊ The Reference Interview: ❊ Connecting Adults to Children's Nonfiction Literature

Patrons come to the reference librarian seeking assistance in locating information of some sort, and the reference interview is one of the most valuable tools that librarians use. It helps both the patron and the librarian determine exactly what the patron's information needs are.

During the reference interview, the librarian:

- ❊ listens to the patron and asks questions to determine the general topic sought,
- ❊ asks the patron additional questions to clarify the patron's true needs and narrow the topic,
- ❊ zeros in on a selection of possible sources, and
- ❊ retrieves possible titles and goes over the contents with the patron to determine whether or not the book(s) would satisfy the patron's needs.

This chapter describes the elements of a successful reference interview and the interpersonal skills the reference librarian should hone. Several case studies demonstrate how these elements have played out in real library situations. The importance of staff training is then addressed.

Elements of a Successful Reference Interview

A reference professional skilled in the interview process is a key component to successfully linking library patrons with the right sources. The success of the reference interview depends on a number of factors, including the following:

- Utilizing both verbal and nonverbal communication to put patrons at ease and encourage interaction and participation

- Asking open-ended questions to get patrons to explain what their needs are; for example, "Can you tell me more about what you are looking for?" or "Could you be more specific about (subject)?"

- Confirming and clarifying the question by restating or paraphrasing it to assure the patron that the librarian is paying attention

- Refraining from asking the patron if he or she has checked the catalog and assuming that the person is skilled in doing so

- If appropriate, explaining the use of the catalog and the library's collections

- Expressing a desire to pursue the hunt for information no matter how difficult the search is

- Matching the subject sought to appropriate titles

- Telling the patron what is being done, such as searching the catalog for specific titles or subject headings

- Avoiding the use of technical terms or jargon, but when they are necessary, clearly explaining what these terms mean

- Asking follow-up questions—for example, "Is the book helpful?" or "Did you find what you were looking for?"

- Inviting the patron to return to the reference desk if the suggested titles are not what they wanted or if the book(s) cannot be located

- Making effective referrals based on in-depth knowledge of other collections

A good reference interview should conclude by encouraging the patron to return if he or she has any other questions or if any problems arise. This reinforces trust and makes the next interview with the user easier to conduct. A good reference interview is not only a positive experience for the patron but it also familiarizes him or her with the interview and search process and thus fosters confidence and makes the patron more comfortable in the library setting—and more likely to return.

Question Negotiation and Case Studies

Even people who are highly competent speaking and reading English can find it difficult to articulate their information needs to a reference librarian; those who aren't so skilled can find it particularly difficult.

Some people are not comfortable admitting that they have a language deficiency or problems with reading comprehension or that they find it hard to voice their needs to a person they don't know. These factors, together with ignorance or befuddlement about a subject or a concept and about how to find books in a library, can cause a patron to be vague or ambiguous. As the reference and research specialist, it is incumbent on the librarian to determine what a patron really wants, to provide accurate and clearly stated responses, and to skillfully guide the patron through the process of retrieving appropriate titles. If the person wants to look for books independently, the librarian should provide clear instructions on how to use the automated catalog effectively and locate books on the shelves. First and foremost, the reference librarian should try to put the patron at ease and make him or her feel comfortable, as well as express an interest in the patron's questions and needs.

Question negotiation is a difficult task, and the librarian should be perceptive and try to "read" patrons' needs by observing body language, facial expressions, and tone of voice while deciding on the best way to probe for pertinent information and clarification of the initial query. A librarian who is friendly, approachable, empathetic, interested, and patient is able to encourage patrons to talk about their information needs and explain why they are looking for material on certain subjects or topical areas, how detailed the information should be (summary, in-depth, etc.), and what reading level is most comfortable for them.

The following case studies of actual reference interviews demonstrate the use of various features of a well-executed reference interview.

Case Study One

"Do you have information on a very large duck
that grows in this country?"

On the surface this question about a super-sized duck seemed vague and preposterous. However, the librarian noted the patron's serious demeanor, foreign accent, and difficulty in expressing his thoughts in English. He was hesitant and embarrassed—but obviously quite serious. As it turned out, he was a recently arrived immigrant who had heard from a friend what he thought was a preposterous story about a fowl bigger than he was, and he was driven to find out if such a creature actually existed. He had failed to understand that his American friend was talking about a famous zoomorphic structure, the Big Duck, which is located on Long Island, in New York State. The reference librarian assured the patron that such a "duck" existed but explained that it was not a living creature. She asked the patron to wait a few minutes and left to retrieve Joan Marie Arbogast's *Buildings in Disguise: Architecture That Looks Like Animals, Food and Other Things* (Honesdale, PA: Boyds Mills Press, 2004: 48 pages) from the children's nonfiction collection.

Fascinated by the strange American architecture, the patron asked if he might take the book to a table to read it and take notes. The librarian asked if he would like to take it home instead. He asked how he might get permission to do so. Because he had appropriate identification, the librarian took him to the circulation desk to apply for a library card. Soon, armed with the card and the borrowed book, the new library user returned to the reference desk, clicked his heels, shook the librarian's hand, and thanked her profusely.

Case Study Two

"I know I'm in the wrong place, but I'll ask anyway...
Who invented kitty litter... and... blue jeans?"

The librarian verified the fact that the patron was in the right place to find answers to his questions. She assured him that no question is considered less important than another and that every effort would be made to quickly locate an appropriate answer. The librarian's informal remark about her own interest in the origins of all sorts of ordinary things relieved the patron's embarrassment. In this case, the librarian was familiar with a particular book that would be a perfect match for the patron, who had stipulated that he wanted only the essential facts. The librarian invited the patron to accompany her to the adult nonfiction section and located Bill Slavin's *Transformed: How Everyday Things Are Made* (Tonawanda, NY: Kids Can Press, 2005: 105 pages) and removed it from the shelf. She flipped to the entry for "kitty litter" and then to "blue jeans" and asked the patron if the information was satisfactory.

Giving an enthusiastic affirmative response, the patron remarked that his appetite for the origins of things was whetted and stated that he wanted to borrow the book to check on the wide assortment of other everyday things it included. Glancing at the cover, he noted the publisher's name, frowned, shrugged and then remarked: "Who cares if it's a kid's publisher... I got what I want and more." After checking the book out, the patron returned to the reference desk, thanked the librarian for her expert help, and commented, "Great idea to put the kid's book in the adult collection!"

Case Study Three

"I'm looking for something about Islam."

The librarian asked the patron if he could tell her more about what he was looking for. To clarify, the patron remarked that he was looking for a short history of Islam but that, after browsing for an hour, he hadn't found anything suitable on the shelves. He added, "I'm curious but not so much that I'd wade through anything more than 100 pages."

When the librarian asked if he had checked the catalog, he seemed to become somewhat unnerved. The librarian assured him that he need only watch while she searched. With further questioning, within the context of informal conversation, the librarian discovered that the reason behind the man's request for a short and, by extension, simple book was the fact that his reading level was below average. The librarian invited the man to accompany her to the adult section. Philip Wilkinson's *Islam* (New York: DK, 2005: 72 pages), rich with captioned illustrations and clear, brief text, was just what the man was looking for. After thanking the librarian, he mentioned that he would surely come back to the reference desk for help. He then proudly remarked that he was on his way to an adult literacy class at the local community college.

Case Study Four

"I'm looking for a relatively concise history of the Civil War.
I've read quite a few detailed histories but I'd like something a
bit less detailed, something to use as a summary, a guide. Oh,
and I'm also looking for the same sort of shorter book that
covers only the Reconstruction Period . . . the social climate
and the changes that occurred."

The librarian admitted to being a Civil War buff and asked the patron if she was too. She responded that things had started out that way but had gradually turned into a graduate research pursuit. The librarian invited the patron to accompany her to the shelves to look for two books that she believed would be ideally suited to the woman's need—Joy Hakim's *War, Terrible War* (New York: Oxford University Press, 2006: 260 pages) and Tonya Bolden's *Cause: Reconstruction America, 1863–1877* (New York: Knopf, 2005: 138 pages). The patron browsed through the two books and remarked that they were perfect, just what she needed.

She hesitated and asked if she would be allowed one more question: "I'm wondering about the Battle of Little Big Horn." She hesitated again and then added, "My guess is I'd have to find something in a research library but I wonder...Do you know of any books that give accounts of the battle from the Indians' point of view?" The librarian knew of one title that was included on a list of books from the children's collection that were recommended for adults. She had ordered it and noticed it had been checked in to be interfiled in the adult American history section. It was Herman J. Viola's *It Is a Good Day to Die: Indian Eyewitnesses Tell the Story of the Battle of Little Big Horn* (New York: Crown, 2001: 101 pages).

The librarian retrieved the book from the shelf and pointed out to the patron that the author, a former director of the National Anthropological Archives, had gathered together excerpts from Native American eyewitness accounts of the battle. The biographical notes, a chronology, and a note on sources were also of interest to the researcher. The patron commented that the book looked like a great "jumping off" source that she had never thought she'd find in the public library collection and that she would be glad to give it a try. The librarian invited her to return to the reference desk at any time and mentioned the reference services available—for example, catalog access, patron referral to special libraries, and interlibrary loan.

Clearly, showing the patron that the reference librarian is available to help, direct, instruct, advise, refer, observe, and provide accurate information in books that meet any user's needs demonstrates competent professional service. Achieving and maintaining a high level of reference service expertise requires ongoing staff training.

Staff Training

Training staff in the art of the reference interview should include a combination of individualized tutoring, observation, and working with experienced reference librarians. This process—tailored to hone the skills needed to provide reference service to those with varying levels of proficiency in reading and speaking English— includes the following:

- Basic training of new staff members in reference service, specifically interview techniques, by looking at how successful interviews transpired via discussion and feedback from experienced professionals

※ Handouts that give tips on conducting effective reference interviews, including methods of engaging with patrons

※ Advanced sessions with experienced reference librarians to teach further refinements of the interview technique

※ Exercises, using case studies recorded by reference librarians engaged in staff training, especially involving difficult queries and hard-to-find titles

※ Ongoing training of both new and experienced reference librarians by repeated analysis of the reference interview process and by identifying methods of improving interview strategies

※ Collaboration with children's librarians to develop a solid knowledge of the range of nonfiction books appropriate for adult use and to acquire expertise in selecting titles that enhance the adult collection

※ Collaboration with ESL and literacy program staff members to develop an understanding of the feelings, attitudes, and problems that ESL and literacy students bring with them to the library

※ Advanced sessions with experienced reference librarians to review the importance of the use of the children's nonfiction collection and to look at recently acquired books and how they fill in the gaps in the adult collection and complement it

※ Training of new staff members in the use of the adult and children's collections, focusing on juvenile nonfiction books that are suitable for adults

Through the staff training process, staff members have an opportunity to analyze the interview process, reinforce and strengthen knowledge of both the adult and children's nonfiction book collections, and evaluate the outcomes of individual patron requests. At the same time, methods of improving interviewing techniques can be efficiently identified and discussed.

Summary

The reference interview is a vital part of the process of connecting library patrons with the informational materials they need. It is both art and science. There are a number of key elements in conducting a successful reference interview, which this chapter has addressed.

Developing expert reference interview skills and establishing good rapport with patrons depend on knowledge, creativity, and the ability to interact well with people, put them at ease, discover what they need, and teach them how to use the library.

Conducting a reference interview with a patron who doesn't speak or read English well can pose special challenges, but their informational needs can be determined using the same interview techniques and interpersonal skills used in interviews with any other patrons. It is important that librarians appreciate what a vital resource the children's nonfiction collection is and that connecting these patrons to these resources can fulfill their informational needs.

A successful connection process also depends on how the adult and children's books are housed (together or separately) and whether or not an ambitious promotion process is in place. These factors are discussed in Chapter 3.

Chapter 3

❈ Housing and Promoting ❈ the Collection: Focusing on Children's Nonfiction

The children's nonfiction collection is generally not the first place that comes to mind as a resource for the adult reading community. In fact, some librarians may fear that by actively promoting the children's nonfiction collection to adults they will bring in more people than they can handle. Considering the limits of their book budget, they are convinced they cannot afford to share the children's collection with adults while continuing to serve children adequately. Their lament: We haven't got enough staff, time, books, or funding to open the juvenile collection to adults.

However, it is important to consider this from a broader perspective. Books that offer such a wealth of information should not remain unknown to the adult population. Keeping them under wraps, so to speak, is a waste of valuable resources and does a disservice to an important segment of the library's patronage. Promoting these resources and thus increasing their use should be viewed as *an asset*. It is a strategic necessity not to view plus-side statistics as a negative. Thus, sharing the collections can be a good business decision.

Adding children's titles to the adult collection will increase the effectiveness of reference service. Economically, a leap in the number of patrons using the library, as well as a jump in circulation figures, would likely result in an increased book budget and possibly additional funding from government, private, and corporate financial sources.

Once the advantages of promoting children's nonfiction are recognized and the decision has been made to move forward, it is time to deal with the logistics. Where will the children's nonfiction collection be housed? Should it be integrated with the adult nonfiction collection, or should it be maintained separately?

Integrating or Separating the Children's Nonfiction Collection

Whether the adult and juvenile nonfiction collections should be integrated or maintained separately is a question that has spurred an ongoing debate over who is better served and who might be short-changed by adopting either approach. There are advantages and disadvantages to both. This chapter provides a basic summary of them. To a great extent, the decision will be dictated by the unique circumstances of the individual library.

The Integrated Nonfiction Collection

In general, integration works well in smaller libraries where the adult and juvenile collections are usually fairly comparable in terms of size. In this case, neither collection is lost within, or overwhelmed by, the other. They are merely blended into one rich collection where titles from one collection complement and augment the other. It represents a case of the whole being more than the sum of its parts.

Librarians who staff libraries of modest to small size that favor nonfiction integration are usually united in citing the advantages of doing so:

- ✖ The integrated collection provides titles covering a wider range of subjects across a wider range of reading abilities, thus expanding its utility to both patrons and the staff members who help them.

- ✖ Service is enhanced because many patrons—both adults and children—find it easier to locate appropriate resources when they are in one central location; thus chances are significantly increased that they will be able to find just what they need.

- Adults seeking nonfiction that is accessible and easy to read can search for appropriate books without experiencing the embarrassment they might feel if they ventured into the separate children's department. This holds true for adults with top-notch reading skills who are simply looking for a basic primer on a topic of interest to them.
- An integrated collection stretches the budget by reducing the number of multiple copies required to adequately serve the needs of both adults and children. When adult and juvenile collections are separate, the children's department must use more of its budget to acquire sufficient multiple copies of titles to satisfy both adult and juvenile users.
- Circulation numbers are likely to increase, because patrons, both assisted and unassisted by the reference librarian, will be more likely to find more titles to check out.
- The nonfiction collection overall will be enhanced and improved, because one rich integrated collection, rather than two smaller, discrete collections, would be in place.

On the other side of the coin, there are some disadvantages in having an integrated nonfiction collection. Many reference librarians—especially those working in large libraries—believe that this practice results in a disservice to children. They reason that when the sole copy of a children's book is borrowed by an adult, children are left with fewer or no choices. Thus, while service to adults may be enhanced, service to children is compromised to the point of inadequacy. Other disadvantages include the following:

- Children may find it difficult to locate appropriate books, which in some cases might be "hidden" among the larger adult books.

✖ Children may have difficulty scanning shelves in a large collection and thus may lose interest and come away empty handed.

✖ Adults might consider the inclusion of children's books added clutter.

✖ Adults might prefer a less crowded area that is free of children.

✖ Adults might be turned off by the noise level children create, and children might be frustrated having to be more quiet than they would in a separate children's department.

✖ Children are perceptive and can sense when they are unwelcome. They may also feel uncomfortable searching for books in the presence of adults, and they may also be less likely to trust the busy reference librarian in the adult section.

✖ Children would have to deal with two points of service because the juvenile reference collection, easy readers, and other materials (e.g., juvenile pamphlets and magazines) would remain housed in the children's department.

Separate Nonfiction Collections

In large libraries, patrons are thought to be better served by providing separate departments dedicated to their age-specific needs. For children, the primary need is for a children's librarian who has the knowledge and expertise to provide reference service and readers' advisory and homework assistance. Children's librarians acquire titles to meet the specific needs of children, not adults, so the budget should be reserved for that *separate* purpose.

Advantages

Advantages of maintaining separate adult and juvenile nonfiction collections include the following:

Advantages for Children

- Children would have access to a children's librarian as well as to the sources needed for homework assignments and other school-related projects. Children are also likely to feel more comfortable with a children's librarian who can best determine their individual reading-level needs.
- Children are better able to locate appropriate books—specific and related—when the books are not mixed in with a myriad of fat adult titles. Thus, the search is less fraught with frustration, and children are more likely to find the experience pleasant and rewarding.

Advantages for Adults

- Adults are likely to prefer to look for books in an area free of the noise and distractions that the presence of children can create.
- A dedicated reference librarian can better serve adults when they are not interrupted by children's "less important," less articulately expressed reference queries.
- Many adults would prefer to search for adult nonfiction titles in a discrete collection free of the "clutter" of intermingled nonadult titles.

Disadvantages

Some librarians balk at the idea of having to educate adult patrons about the benefits of examining both nonfiction collections as potential resources. They feel that this places an extra burden on them. They also worry that referring an adult to the children's department might be perceived as an insult. This latter situation can be easily avoided, however. If the librarian determines during the reference interview that the best resource for an adult is in the children's collection, she or he can simply retrieve the book while the patron waits. The reference interview would then continue as the librarian explains the appropriateness of the book(s) for the patron's individual needs. This is a simple solution, although it is more time-consuming for the librarian.

Among the other disadvantages of maintaining separate nonfiction collections are the following:

- Additional copies of certain children's titles must be purchased for the juvenile collection to accommodate requests from the children as well as requests from adult users. This strains the budget allocated to the children's department.
- Without one central location, the search is more involved, with a greater chance that an excellent resource will be overlooked.
- The chances decrease that patrons will find more titles on a subject or aspect of a subject.
- When the adult nonfiction collection lacks sufficient book choices for adults with low reading levels and juvenile alternatives are not an option, it falls short in its ability to serve all of its patrons well.

Transitional Titles

In large libraries, where the collections are separate, it is beneficial to have transitional titles in both the adult and the children's collections. As adults and children move beyond the early stages of reading, they require books that support their transition toward understanding more complex language. Transitional titles are more challenging to read for those not yet ready for full-length adult books or more complex juvenile reading levels. Transitional books are usually about 100 pages in length, have easy-to-read type faces, and present a challenge without intimidation. Books considered transitional have fewer illustrations and more detailed explications of subjects such as history, science, and biography. This arrangement requires duplication of some titles and thus shrinks the budget available to purchase other titles.

Regardless of how the children's nonfiction collection is housed, there is no question that adult reference librarians should be aware of what the juvenile collection has to offer. They should familiarize themselves with the children's titles that they feel would augment the adult collection. Most important, they should actively promote the children's nonfiction collection to patrons whose information needs could effectively be satisfied by it.

Promoting Children's Nonfiction

To build public awareness of the wide range of nonfiction sources available to adults, as well as of the quality and commitment of the reference service in place in libraries, a variety of promotional methods should be considered. These include traditional printed and visual promotional vehicles, such as the following:

- *Newsletters:* For patrons to feel good about their library experience, it must be easy and rewarding for them to look for books that suit their needs, interests, and reading levels. Newsletters for current and potential patrons can focus on children's nonfiction titles by providing short bibliographies on specific subjects or topical areas, as well as reviews of newly acquired titles—and this can be done without identifying them as having been written for a juvenile audience.

- *Bookmarks:* Everyone loves to get a free bookmark, and one that promotes books that are a solid source of information on a variety of subjects serves as a reminder to the public that the library should be the first place they look for books that fit their interests and reading levels.

- *Brochures and posters:* Brochures and posters, too, can be used effectively to promote the features and merits of the children's nonfiction titles within the adult collection, as well as the reference services available in the nonfiction section of the library.

✖ *Flyers:* Flyers are excellent vehicles for providing information about newly acquired titles that complement and update the collection (including children's titles not identified as such). Flyers can be used to promote workshops on using the library's reference service, navigating the library's Web site, searching its catalog, locating appropriate titles on its shelves, and so forth.

✖ *Exhibits and displays:* Exhibits and displays can highlight nonfiction titles that provide concise explications of popular subjects without noting that they are children's titles. They can be located within the library and outside.

These promotional vehicles are fairly inexpensive to produce. Printed promotional materials should be available at reference desks in the various library departments, as well as outside the library in school libraries, academic libraries, ESL and adult literacy teaching facilities, social service agencies, higher education facilities where literacy and reading are taught, in local stores (e.g., in windows and on counters), and anywhere else that is frequented by the library's target audience.

The Internet also provides excellent promotional opportunities in the form of Web sites and online catalogs. An engaging library Web site is an important means of communicating information to both current and prospective library patrons. It is a tool with which the library can advertise its services and provide information about its collections. It has the power to improve the library's image and allows the library to offer enhanced services. Some of its features might include the following:

✖ Lists of new titles by subject

✖ A list of reference services

✖ Bibliographies on particular subjects or aspects of subjects

✖ A virtual library tour

✖ Announcements of programs and workshops on various topics

⌖ Instructions for using the catalog

⌖ Lists of the special collections available

⌖ Instructions for searching online databases

⌖ A database of community information services

⌖ Links to definitions of terms and concepts

⌖ Discussions of subjects or authors

⌖ Links to databases searchable through the library

⌖ Access to free remote Internet sites

If the Web site includes an e-mail link allowing individuals to contact the library directly, patrons and prospective patrons can submit questions from a remote location. They will thus be free to ask questions that they might be reluctant to ask in person.

The Web site can be updated periodically to feature information about specific library collections, workshops on how to use the catalog, new acquisitions, reference services, library tours, and so on. Highlighted boxes might list children's nonfiction titles that meet the informational, educational, recreational, and cultural needs of adult users, especially those who are new to the United States and/or those who are taking courses in adult literacy or ESL.

Online catalogs are another effective promotional tool. They enable patrons to research and locate materials in the collection(s). It is searchable by author, title, subject, and keyword. Advanced searching allows for modifying searches by date, date range, word stems, word proximity, illustrator, and other bibliographic information. The electronic catalog might include links to book award lists, bestsellers in adult and juvenile nonfiction, and Web sites of interest for related material on the subject(s) being researched.

Other factors important to promotion include the following one-on-one opportunities that allow librarians and their colleagues to promote the library and its resources through interpersonal communications:

⌖ *Outreach programs:* Children's nonfiction books should be promoted both inside the library and outside. Outside efforts can be made at community meetings; at ESL and adult literacy classes; during book talks; as part of outreach service to special groups, such as new Americans; in adult literacy departments; at social service agencies; as part of adult new learner programs, and so forth. Presentations by library staff members allow people to ask questions about the collection and about what the reference librarian can do to help connect them to appropriate sources. Promotional materials can be handed out, and an invitation to visit the library and talk to the librarians can be extended.

- *Orientation sessions:* Knowledge of the location and purpose of the reference desk, the location of the catalog, and the arrangement and content of the nonfiction collection(s) are a must for new library users. Rather than floundering around the library, patrons can gain an immediate understanding of where things are and what the library has to offer.
- *Workshops:* Workshops can provide information about reference service. Emphasis should be placed on the essentials—how to use the catalog, how to use reference sources and other resources available, such as children's nonfiction titles. Workshops can be basic instructional sessions as well as refresher courses. Small group (two to four people) sessions should be available to anyone as an alternative to the larger, more practical, group workshops. Reference librarians must tailor instruction to fit patron comprehension ability, interest, and level of need—anywhere from basic facts to more complex data in both print and online sources. The benefit of workshops to the library include more knowledgeable users, increased use of reference services, and greater use of the library as the first place to go to locate information of all sorts.

In the end, however, nothing is as important as the one-on-one relationship the librarian establishes with his or her patrons. Good patron relationships are of paramount importance if reference librarians are to provide superlative service—defining the reference query, locating the books that hit the mark, and providing appropriate information at the correct reading level. Librarians need to be professional and respond to individual requests as best they can, establishing a personal relationship, reacting positively, encouraging and empathetically prodding patrons to explain their true needs, and sticking with patrons until they are connected with the books that answer their questions.

Summary

Juvenile nonfiction is no longer just for children. Where the children's nonfiction collection is housed—whether the adult and juvenile nonfiction collections are integrated or maintained separately—depends on the unique circumstances of the individual library. There are advantages and disadvantages to both approaches. In general, integration tends to work best in smaller libraries, while maintaining separate collections is thought to be the best option for large libraries.

Regardless of whether the collections are blended or separated, reference librarians must be aware of children's nonfiction titles and actively promote their use. There are numerous promotional methods—printed, electronic, and interpersonal—that can be used effectively.

Promotion of children's nonfiction titles (along with the quality of reference service) will help to (1) increase patron and potential patron knowledge of the wealth of resources housed in the library, (2) increase adult use of appropriate juvenile sources, (3) increase knowledge of reference service and resources among those who traditionally do not use libraries, and (4) increase use of the library as the first place to go to fulfill information needs.

Part II

❋ Recommended ❋ Titles: An Annotated Bibliography

Architecture

Arbogast, Joan Marie. ***Buildings in Disguise: Architecture That Looks Like Animals, Food, and Other Things.*** Honesdale, PA: Boyds Mills Press, 2004.

Pages: 48
Series: —

This enjoyable book provides a satisfying look at mimetic architecture and takes the reader on a tour of buildings scattered around the United States that look like ducks, elephants, beagles, and roosters; gas stations shaped like tepees, pagodas, teapots, and shells; lodgings shaped like pueblos, teepees, windmills, and boats; restaurants shaped like giant milk bottles, puppies, watermelons, teapots, mini castles, ice cream cones, and sombreros; entertainment complexes built like a palace, a giant coaster wagon, a thermometer, an oversized shoe; and office buildings that look like a giant bureau with socks hanging from a drawer, a bulldozer, a miner's hat, a giant basket, and a pair of binoculars. There is a chapter on the future of mimetic architecture and a one-page epilogue on saving these structures.

Two chapters are devoted to the famous zoomorphic structures Lucy, the Margate Elephant (Margate, New Jersey), built in 1881 and designated a National Historic Landmark in 1976; and The Big Duck (Flanders, Long Island, New York), built in 1931, saved from demolition in 1987, and placed on the National Register of Historic Places.

Reproductions of period photos, prints, postcards, as well as more recent photos of the sites, most in striking full color, and fact boxes on selected structures complement the clear and concise text.

A map of the United States, indicating the locations of the 24 buildings mentioned in the text, is printed on the endpapers.

This book is a fun browsing title, as well as a useful primary source of information on inventive architecture.

Glossary: No
Bibliography: Yes, of books, informational brochures, and Web
    sites
Index: Yes
Level: Beginning–Intermediate New Readers

Lynch, Anne. *Great Buildings.* New York: Barnes & Noble, 2005.

Pages: 64
Series: Discoveries

Twenty-six of the world's greatest structures are presented chrono-logically on double-page spreads and one four-page spread. They include a Trobriand woven hut; a Mayan pyramid in Mexico; Ishtar Gate, Babylon; the Baths of Caracalla; a Hindu temple in India; a Buddhist shrine in Indonesia; the Hall of Supreme Harmony in Bejing; Horyuji Temple Complex in Japan; Hagia Sophia, Turkey; the Alhambra, Spain; a Norwegian stave church; Conway castle, Wales; Notre Dame Cathedral, Paris; Rome's St.Peter's Basilica; Casa Mila in Barcelona; the Toronto SkyDome; and the Sydney Opera House. The architectural styles and elements used are described against a background of religious and cultural influ-ences. Chock-full of information, there are numerous boxes explaining related concepts such as brick making, corbelled roofs, the development of the arch, the function of beams and brackets, and what prestressed concrete is. Full-color large and smaller photographs and drawings fill each page. Many are cutaway views showing construction, with pointers to interesting aspects of the various structures. The final double-page spread contains a world map showing the locations of the structures featured in the book. The brief text, enhanced by detailed illustrations, takes the reader on a guided tour of the exterior and interior details of these great buildings. The book provides readers with a solid survey of the history of architecture.

Glossary: Yes
Bibliography: No
Index: Yes
Level: Beginning–Intermediate New Readers

Macaulay, David. *Building Big.* New York: Walter Lorraine Books/Houghton Mifflin, 2000.

Pages: 192
Series: —

Why choose one shape over others? Why choose one building material and not another? Why choose one site instead of another? Macaulay's questions led him to examine the basic design process, which, he states, begins with engineers and architects identifying problems they must solve as they plan a construction project. "Once we recognize that the elements of common sense and logic are at least as important a role . . . as imagination and technical know-how, even the biggest things we build can be brought down to size." The author has indeed brought his survey of the history and building of the biggest of all structures (bridges, tunnels, dams, domes, and skyscrapers), as well as the rather daunting engineering problems related to planning and building big, down to size. He effectively uses concise language infused with intelligence and humor, as can be seen in his introduction to tunnels, for example: "While bridges, skyscrapers, domes and even a few dams enjoy varying amounts of popularity, I think it is fairly safe to say that only an engineer could love a tunnel."

Macaulay romps around the world and through the centuries, taking readers on a close-up tour of such structures as Rome's Ponte Fabricio, Scotland's Firth of Fourth, Boston's Big Dig, New York's World Trade Center, and Kuala Lumpur's Petronas Towers. Subtle humor appears in his cutaway views and diagrams: a friendly sea monster pops out of the water to inspect the Firth of

Forth construction; a caption below the Holland Tunnel reads, "Are you sure this is the way to France?"; one of a pair of mice sitting on the English side of the Chunnel notes that "cheese" becomes "fromage" at the other end. Delightful fun, these little surprises make the reader pay more attention to the details. The integration of text and illustrations effectively spotlights design objectives, the interrelationships of structure and environment, and the engineering solutions used to complete the structures.

A companion to the PBS series of the same name, *Building Big* has a narrower focus and stands on its own. Macaulay's expertise combining engaging narrative and a strikingly clear presentation of facts makes this title remarkable.

Glossary: Yes.
Bibliography: No
Index: No
Level: Intermediate–Advanced New Readers

Macaulay, David. *Unbuilding*. Boston: Houghton Mifflin, 1987.

Pages: 78
Series: —

Using a unique combination of fiction and nonfiction, Macaulay captures the feeling of emptiness a demolished famous building leaves in the city and in the minds and hearts of its caring residents. This mature, contemporary satire criticizes those who would let the building go to a wealthy and influential foreigner with the power to take away a city's most precious landmark. Macaulay beautifully illustrates (in precise black-and-white line drawings) the methods and equipment used to unbuild the Empire State Building. The story of oil-rich Prince Ali, who succeeds in acquiring the landmark, intending to carry it away and re-erect it in the Arabian dessert as the headquarters of his nation's Institute of Petroleum, focuses on the importance of preserving landmarks while they still exist. The beauty and architectural details of the Empire State Building, as well as the void left in the city and its famous skyline by its unbuilding, is vividly demonstrated in this memorable book.

Glossary: Yes, of architectural terms
Bibliography: No
Index: No
Level: Intermediate–Advanced New Readers

Maddex, Diane and Roxie Munro. *Architects Make Zigzags: Looking at Architecture from A to Z.* Illustrated by Roxie Munro. Hoboken, NJ: John Wiley, 1995.

Pages: 64
Series: —

Munro's detailed line drawings capture the essence of the 26 terms defined in this unique architectural dictionary. The letter "A" defines the architect's job: to give form to ideas and guide others in the process of executing these ideas to create a wide variety of features, including brackets, columns, eaves, facades, ironwork, keystones, newel posts, quoins, roofs, verandas, and zigzags. Some basic facts about the buildings are listed in the back of the book. The illustrations offer a brief glance at 300 years of American architectural design from the House of Seven Gables in Salem, Massachusetts (1668), to the zigzag design in the lobby of the General Electric Building (1931) in New York City. Two entries ("P" and "X") refer to the importance of preserving landmarks and old buildings and the use of X-ray to examine the interior of wood and walls to determine their condition without destroying the structure.

This is a mature alphabet book appropriate for adults with an interest in building design.

Glossary: No
Bibliography: Yes
Index: No
Level: Beginning New Readers

Mattern, Joanne. *Homes.* Detroit: Gale Group, 2004.

Pages: 32
Series: Yesterday and Today

This history of dwellings consists of 14 double-page chapters that include up to four paragraphs of basic background information, boxes with related facts to supplement the text, and clearly labeled and captioned pictures and photographs. The reader is given a quick run through of the history of architecture from prehistoric times, ancient Egypt and the Middle East, ancient Greece and Rome, ancient China, pre-medieval times, the Maya in Central America, castles in Medieval Europe, and on to the Industrial Revolution, the American frontier, and present-day modern homes. A time line runs down the right margins to remind the reader of the years covered in each chapter. Clearly and concisely written, this book is a worthwhile quick survey of the history of homes.

Glossary: Yes
Bibliography: Yes, of books and Web sites
Index: Yes
Level: Beginning–Intermediate New Readers

Rubin, Susan Goldman. *There Goes the Neighborhood: Ten Buildings People Love to Hate.* New York: Holiday House, 2001.

Pages: 96
Series: —

This title provides a fascinating look at ten beloved buildings that were at first despised as eyesores. Attacked verbally as well as with fruit and stones, they were hated because they were uniquely different or wildly original. The Washington Monument, the tallest masonry structure in the world and likened to a stalk of asparagus, endured over a century of constant criticism as it was completed. The useless and monstrous Eiffel Tower, "the dishonor of Paris," became a symbol of the city and the country once the pieces of the giant iron erector set were put together. Other reviled buildings included are the Flat

Iron Building in New York City; Philip Johnson's glass house in New Canaan, Connecticut; Frank O. Gehry's house in Santa Monica, California; Neuschwanstein Castle in Hohenschwangau, Germany, and its replica, Sleeping Beauty Castle in Anaheim, California; New York City's Solomon R. Guggenheim Museum; the Pompidou Center in Paris; The Walker Community Library, Minneapolis, Minnesota; and the golden arched McDonald's worldwide. Rubin fills the narrative with quotes and critical comments from artists, architects, writers, journalists, poets, and residents who reviled the intrusive structures.

Pictures and architectural drawings reminiscent of blueprints complement the text. The book is printed in blue type, with occasional pages white on blue, to complete the architect's blueprint look. Notes on some of the architects and a list of organizations for further information on the subject are included.

Rubin offers a glimpse into the long history of each structure and reveals a bit of each architect's creative process. This title is well researched and offers a nontraditional, mature approach to architecture, changing styles and tastes, as well as public opinion.

Glossary: Yes
Bibliography: Yes, including books, videocassettes, interviews, Web sites
Index: Yes
Level: Intermediate–Advanced New Readers

Sullivan, George. *Built to Last: Building America's Amazing Bridges, Dams, Tunnels, and Skyscrapers.* New York: Scholastic, 2005.

Pages: 128
Series: —

A fascinating look at the design and construction of 17 architectural and engineering wonders, this book surveys American building, the ingenuity and determination behind each project, and the technological accomplishments related to each structure. Construction projects, from the nation's earliest days to the present, are presented in chronological order and include the Erie Canal, the Capitol, The Flat Iron Building, Transcontinental Railroad, Empire State Building, Hoover Dam, the U.S. interstate highway system, Chesapeake Bay Bridge, the Central Artery Tunnel Project (Boston's Big Dig), and City Tunnel No. 3 (New York). A number of fact boxes provide details on a variety of related subjects, such as the construction of dams, a look inside a caisson, and the impact of electric elevators on the working conditions of the builders of skyscrapers.

Archival photographs and engravings, architectural drawings, color photos (many printed horizontally across a double-page spread) provide a full view of each project. Sullivan integrates economic and social history in this impressive, well-written, and beautifully designed title.

Glossary: No
Bibliography: Yes
Index: Yes
Level: Intermediate–Advanced New Readers

Zaunders, Bo. *Gargoyles, Girders & Glass Houses.* Illustrated by Roxie Munro. New York: Dutton Children's Books, 2004.

Pages: 48
Series: —

The first stop on this impressive architectural tour of five centuries and six countries is Florence, Italy, at Filippo Brunelleschi's (1377–1446) cathedral dome of Santa Maria del Flore. The reader then continues on to the mosques of Mimar Koca Sinan (1489–1588) in Turkey; Brazil and it's great sculptor and architect Antonio Francisco Lisboa (the Little Cripple, 1738–1814) at work on his statue of the Prophet Jonah; Brooklyn, New York's Brooklyn Bridge and the Roebling family (1806–1903); Paris' Eiffel Tower and Alexandre-Gustave Eiffel (1832–1923), the builder of the iron wonder; Antoni Gaudi (1852–1926) of Barcelona, the designer of Jose Batllo's colorful and curvy house; and finally back to New York to look at the graceful Chrysler Building, designed by William Van Alen (1883–1954). Each chapter begins with a discussion of significant segments of the master builders' lives and then provides historical and architectural background while revealing the passion behind their creations. Munro's mix of full-page and smaller drawings convey both the subtle details and the grandeur of the structures described. The combination of lively writing and dramatic illustrations makes this book a unique and thoroughly satisfying introduction to architecture.

Glossary: No
Bibliography: Yes
Index: No
Level: Beginning–Intermediate New Readers

❈ The Arts (Art, Music, Film, ❈ Theater, and Dance)

Ardley, Neil. *Eyewitness Music.* New York: DK, 2004.

Pages: 72
Series: Eyewitness

Clear, concise text and informative captions accompany high-quality photographs, cutaways, and diagrams in this comprehensive survey of music. An introduction to sound precedes short sections on families of instruments: wind, pipes and flutes, hybrids, brass, strings, percussion— followed by a look at electrifying music and machine music. The history and development of the different instruments, how they produce sound, how they are constructed, and what their appeal is are traced. The book also includes an illustrated section on fascinating facts, four questions and answers, a short list of "record breakers," a two-page who's who of major composers, and a list of places to visit. Chock-full of facts, the book is of interest to readers from children through adults.

Glossary: Yes, including a survey of musical styles
Bibliography: Yes, of Web sites
Index: Yes
Level: Beginning–Intermediate New Readers

Barber, Nicola. *The World of Music.* London: Evans Brothers, 2000.

Pages: 94
Series: —

In less than 100 pages the author provides a comprehensive look at the world of music. Excellent illustrations include pictures, photographs, charts, and diagrams. Color-coded boxes provide additional information throughout the text. The first four chapters discuss string, wind, percussion, and electronic instruments. The positions of the instruments within an orchestra are indicated on small, color-coded diagrams of a full orchestra. Keyboard diagrams show the range of each instrument. A "Listen Out For" section identifies particular works of music in which each of the instruments is featured. The next four chapters trace the history of the music of the Western world, from 1100 AD to modern times. Each chapter begins with a time line that compares musical developments with events in history. "Key Fact" sections provide supplementary information. The history of folk music and definitions of pulse and rhythm and pitch and melody are included. This is an authoritative, well-organized, and richly illustrated reference source.

Glossary: Yes, of musical terms and of composers
Bibliography: No
Index: Yes
Level: Intermediate New Readers

Bolton, Linda. Impressionism. New York: Peter Bedrick Books, 2000.

Pages: 32
Series: Art Revolutions

A brief overview of Impressionism, a revolution in color and form, is followed by a glimpse of ten leading artists, and two or three good-quality reproductions of their works, including Monet, Renoir, Pissarro, Sisley, Manet, Morisot, Cassatt, Cailebotte, and Van Gogh. The distinctive characteristics of each piece, and their importance to this art movement, are concisely explained. The double-page chapters include biographical data, commentary, and added bits of information in sidebars. The book concludes with a two-page section on other artists influenced by the Impressionist use of bright color and broken brushwork—Whistler, Gauguin, Cezanne, and Seurat. A reproduction of one painting for each artist accompanies the text.

This book is memorable for its clearly written presentation of a complex subject. It serves as a quick review of the subject as well as a lead-in to more in-depth research.

Glossary: Yes
Bibliography: Yes, of galleries to visit, Web sites, and books; includes a time line
Index: Yes
Level: Beginning New Readers

Cross, Robin. *Movie Magic: A Behind-the-Scenes Look at Filmmaking.* Minneapolis: Sagebrush, 1996.

Pages: 62
Series: —

This title gives readers an up-close, behind-the-scenes look at moviemaking from Edison's film *Fred Ott's Sneeze* (1894) to the present. Short chapters look at the early years of the film industry; studios and stars; comedy and thrillers (continuity, storyboards, and directing); cameras and cameramen; horror (production design, makeup, and lighting); war and westerns (location shooting, props, and extras); stunt artists; historical epics (glass painting, wardrobe, and sets); the big screen; musicals (sound and sound effects); science fiction (model making, special effects, and animatronics); the role of computers; animation (computer animation and claymation); and postproduction activity. Cross answers a number of questions about the movie industry—with mention of selected films and actors. Rich with illustration, and images of filmstrips used for sidebars, the book serves as an excellent introduction to the making of American movies.

A double-page movie game might be of interest to some older readers as well as to children.

Glossary: No
Bibliography: No
Index: Yes
Level: Intermediate New Readers

Finley, Carol. *The Art of African Masks: Exploring Cultural Traditions.* Minneapolis: Lerner, 1999.

Pages: 64
Series: Art Around the World

Masks were originally much more than the decorative art objects now found in museums. African masks were used for ceremonial and religious purposes and represent spirits, legendary animals, or mythological beings. Artistically stunning, their purpose was to hide the identity of the wearer by covering either the face or the head to create a new image from the spirit world during religious or ritual performances to ensure abundant crops or fertility, for example.

The introduction to masks mentions those used in other cultures as well: ancient Greeks and Romans played some roles wearing masks; the Japanese and Chinese still use them in traditional the-ater; a pair of masks, comic and tragic, symbolize drama in Western civilization; Tibetans make them to scare away demons; the Hopi Indians of the southwestern United States use "kachinas" to repre-sent helpful spirits; and masks are traditionally worn on Halloween, Carnival, and Mardi Gras. However, the wide range of imagery, tech-nique, and style found in African masks is unmatched in any other culture or country.

Color coded by regions—West Africa and the Guinea Coast, Western Sudan, Central Africa—the book provides a brief history and explanation of the culture of each area along with the discus-sion of the masks. A map of ethnic groups in Africa is included. Finley notes that information on African ethnic groups is incom-plete and that the traditional way of life has disappeared. As a result, masks are now made for collectors and tourists. The color photo illustrations, both small and full-page, are striking.

Glossary: No
Bibliography: Yes
Index: Yes
Level: Intermediate New Readers

Fiscus, James W. *Meet King Kong*. New York: Rosen, 2005.

Pages: 48
Series: Famous Movie Monsters

With illustrations from the 1933 movie *King Kong* to support the text, Fiscus begins the book by outlining the King Kong story. Chapter 2 traces the making of the 1933 movie: script writing, cast, production, stop-motion animation, special effects, and information on the film's budget. The origins of King Kong are examined in Chapter 3: the influence of early epics and adventures (from the *Odyssey* to such "ape" movies as *The Murders in the Rue Morgue*, 1914 and 1932 films; Burroughs's *Tarzan of the Apes*, first filmed in 1918; to *The Lost World*, 1925). Also included is a bit on the influence of the real adventures behind King Kong, as experienced by three of its creators—Merian C. Cooper, Ernest Schoedsack, and Schoedsack's wife, screenwriter Ruth Rose. The final chapter looks at the phenomenon of *King Kong*, which opened March 2, 1933, and was released a month later. Some scenes considered too graphic were censored and cut in 1938 but were restored in the 1970s. These are available on the 60th anniversary VHS tape and on the 2005 DVD, released to coincide with Peter Jackson's new version of the film. Fiscus points out that remakes and spin-offs, such as *Son of Kong* and *Mighty Joe Young*, never enjoyed the success of the original movie. The author concludes that, although the academic and social critics read more into *Kong* than what it was, the film has always been simply a well-conceived, entertaining movie.

A filmography and various fact boxes are included. Yes, this title has the look of a book for young children, but the language is not simplistic. It is a good summary of the story and history of the original *King Kong* movie that will not insult the adult reader.

Glossary: No
Bibliography: Yes, of Web sites, VHS, DVDs, and books
Index: Yes
Level: Intermediate New Readers

Langley, Andrew. *Shakespeare's Theatre.* Oxford: Oxford University Press, 1999.

Pages: 48
Series: —

This is an engaging description of the rebuilding of Shakespeare's Globe Theatre, an ambitious project inspired and led by American actor and film director Sam Wanamaker. The book also includes a history of the growth of English theater, as well as that of the original Globe Theatre, and Shakespeare's role as actor, playwright, and sharer in the Globe. June Everett's detailed paintings of every stage of the new Globe Theatre project, along with paintings of the original Globe and its performances and audience, make this book a treat. A list of important dates in Shakespeare's life, a list of plays in approximate order of first performance, the main London theaters in Shakespeare's time, and a paragraph of information on the new Globe Theatre follow the text.

Glossary: No
Bibliography: No
Index: Yes
Level: Intermediate–Advanced New Readers

Mason, Antony. *Music.* Broomall, PA: Mason Crest, 2003.

Pages: 40
Series: Culture Encyclopedia

In a short introduction, Mason talks about the appeal of music, the most popular and widespread art form. The next chapter discusses ancient instruments: the painted pottery drums of the Nazca of Peru; the Egyptian bow harp; the tambourine; the Mayan pottery

whistle; panpipes, named after the Greek god Pan; and the didgeri-
doo of the Australian Aborigines. A fact box defines the first instrument, the human voice. Subsequent double-page chapters provide
brief overviews of percussion, wind, stringed, and keyboard instruments; hybrid instruments such as the saxophone, accordion, and
one-man band; the voice, from Elton John to "the three tenors"
(Pavarotti, Domingo, Carreras) to musicals, gospel music, and rap;
playing together—solo musicians, an orchestra, jazz, folk, and
marching band; composers and composing music (written music
and computer composition; classical music; improvisation, such as
Dixieland, rock music, and rhythm and blues; and recorded music)
from Caruso to Madonna; the music industry; and, finally, world
music. Each chapter has a fact box with a tidbit of related information. The book is rich with illustrations that complement the text in
this clearly written overview of a fascinating topic.

Glossary: Yes
Bibliography: No
Index: Yes
Level: Beginning New Readers

**Merlo, Claudio. *The History of Art from Ancient to Modern
Times.*** Lincolnwood, IL: Peter Bedrick, 2000.

Pages: 124
Series: Masters of Art

Merlo took on the challenge to present a comprehensive overview
of the greatest achievements in the history of art, from cave paintings
to medieval art, the Renaissance, Impressionism, classical sculpture,
and on to modern times. The reader is taken on a richly illustrated,
full-color tour of Asia, North and South America, Europe, Africa,
and the Pacific for a glimpse of the various religious and cultural
influences on artistic styles and techniques noted in various parts of
the world. Merlo also visits the world's most renowned sculptors,
painters, and architects and provides short bits of information on
them. The book includes photos of works of art, along with comments

on the personal and political influences on each creation and definitions of artistic methods, such as fresco, bark painting, and mosaic. Cutaways highlight architectural wonders, artists and sculptors at work in studios, great buildings, and the outdoors. Merlo's ambitious goal allows only brief text,but, along with the many detailed illustrations, this title is noteworthy.

Glossary: No
Bibliography: No
Index: Yes
Level: Beginning New Readers

Muhlberger, Richard. *What Makes a Monet a Monet?* New York: Viking, 2002.

Pages: 48
Series: What Makes A . . . ?

This introduction to Monet begins with a photograph of the 18-year-old aspiring artist and a three-page biographical sketch. Short analyses of a small selection of his paintings are accompanied by full-color reproductions that include information on what inspired Monet to paint them, their style and composition, the technique used, and an interpretation of each. The unique qualities of Monet's technique that defines the artist's reputation are summarized. This excellent, intelligently written exploration of Monet is one volume in an impressive series that includes books on Bruegel, Degas, Raphael, Rembrandt, and Van Gogh.

Glossary: No
Bibliography: No
Index: No
Level: Beginning New Readers

Paul, Ann Whitford. *Seasons Sewn: A Year in Patchwork.*
Illustrated by Michael McCurdy. New York: Harcourt Children's Books, 2000.

Pages: 37
Series: —

A brief introduction describes what life during the four seasons would have been like for an early American country child within 100 years after the Declaration of Independence. During this historical period, mothers usually spent their evenings doing fine sewing, that is, embroidery, crewel work, and patchwork quilting. The stories behind each named pattern are presented and illustrated with lively pictures that depict life from spring through winter. A single quilt square and a pattern of four squares are shown in watercolor drawings. At the end of the book the author wonders what stories told in newly created patterns would reveal about modern life. This is an unusual and enchanting book in which the history of frontier and pioneer life is explained through patchwork.

Glossary: No
Bibliography: Yes
Index: No
Level: Beginning New Readers

Peppin, Anthea. *Nature in Art.* New York: Houghton Mifflin, 1992.

Pages: 48
Series: —

This book provides a fine lesson in art appreciation by examining how various artists transfer what they see in nature to canvas and focusing on certain details to point out techniques used by different artists. Examples include the still life of fruits and flowers of the Dutch artist Jan van Huysum, which is so realistic that the viewer might want to touch and smell the flowers and eat the grapes, and the pleasing designs of the Japanese artist, Kitagawa Utamaro. Peppin discusses how different artists captured the movement of wind and water, the power of nature or of natural disaster, made pigments from natural substances, used warm and cold colors to capture the mood of a scene, created animal patterns, painted a scene of nature from imagination, and used nature's shapes, patterns, and designs. There are two-page sections on block prints, line drawings of animals, animal portraits, Aboriginal bark pictures, and totem poles. A look at art materials and short biographies of the artists mentioned in the text complete the book. Various art projects, based on the ideas and techniques of the artists mentioned in each section, might be challenging for adults interested in learning how to create their own art works.

Glossary: No
Bibliography: No
Index: Yes, with page references to paintings in italics
Level: Intermediate New Readers

Thomas, Roger. *Keyboards.* Chicago: Heineman Library, 2002.

Pages: 32
Series: Soundbites

This title briefly introduces the origin and development of the keyboard from the ancient Egyptian hydraulis to the modern digital keyboard. Concise definitions of types of keyboard instruments and how they work are followed by double-page chapters on the piano, the harpsicord family, the clavicord, the pipe organ, reed organs, early synthesizers, polyphonic synthesizers, samplers and workstations, computers, and music and other innovative types of keyboards. Fact boxes provide related information of interest. The book is richly illustrated with photographs and a few clear diagrams. Mature language written for the older child and teen reader makes this an excellent ready-reference source for adults. Other titles in the series include *Brass, Percussion, Strings, Woodwind,* and *Groups, Bands, & Orchestras.*

Glossary: Yes
Bibliography: Yes, of three titles
Index: Yes
Level: Beginning New Readers

Topal, Cathy Weisman. *Children and Painting.* Worcester, MA: Davis, 1992.

Pages: 168
Series: —

Why would a textbook on teaching painting to children be appropriate for adults? As the author states, the basics of learning how to paint are the same for aspiring artists of any age.

Designed to help teachers to interest children in painting, this book gradually introduces particular concepts and techniques at their simplest levels. Once one basic concept is understood and a technique mastered, new ones are suggested to further challenge the beginning artist.

The text is divided into four parts: the first part discusses approaches to painting (exploring the basics of brushstrokes, texture, shape, color, mixing tints, and composition); the second part concentrates on subjects and themes (flowers and still life, the environment, animals, and people); part three is devoted to alternative approaches and aesthetics (black ink painting of East Asia and watercolors); and the final part covers thinking about the painting process (improving the painting process through evaluation, matting and displaying, etc.; understanding paints and painting supplies; and practicing the cleaning-up routine). The clearly written text is enhanced with step-by-step visual instructions for each project and activity. There are excellent photographs of paintings done by children and well-known artists to demonstrate various techniques. Chapter summaries are also included.

Glossary: Yes
Bibliography: Yes
Index: Yes
Level: Beginning–Intermediate New Readers

Tythacott, Louise. *Dance.* New York: Raintree, 1995.

Pages: 48
Series: Traditions Around the World

Tythacott states that every culture has a tradition of dance, which may be an early form of communication. Dances express a variety of emotions and hopes for good luck in life, health, war, and so forth. They are often an important part of religious practice or magic to conjure rain, a bountiful harvest, or spirits. Whatever the origins are of the world's many folk dances, they undoubtedly entertain. The derivation, history, meaning, and costumes of dances of the peoples of Europe, North America, Central and South America, Asia, Africa, and the Pacific are discussed. Each section begins with an outline map of the world that highlights the continent featured. Photographs bring the colorful costumes and dancers to life. The combination of an informative text and attractive format offers an enjoyable introduction to folk dance.

Glossary: Yes
Bibliography: Yes
Index: Yes
Level: Beginning New Readers

Whiting, Jim. *Auguste & Louis Lumiere and the Rise of Motion Pictures.* Hockessin, DE: Mitchell Lake, 2005.

Pages: 48
Series: Uncharted, Unexplored and Unexplained Scientific
     Advancements of the 19th Century

In 1995, the same year that *Toy Story* (the first totally computer-animated feature film), *Jumanjii* (which used computer-generated special effects), and *Braveheart* (which used computer animation to show battle scenes) were introduced, 40 of the world's most famous movie directors collaborated on the film *Lumiere and Company*. They made it to honor the 100th anniversary of the first commercial movie exhibition of 1895. The brother's original Lumiere camera was used—it had to be kept in one position; the films could be only about 50 seconds long; and there was no sound. The author notes that the Lumiere brothers were also responsible for innovations in color still photography. Chapter 2 presents biographical data on the Lumieres, discusses the creative process that led to the invention of their camera, the Cinematographe, and the films they made to demonstrate the camera's capabilities.

George Melies saw the possibilities of the camera, bought a similar one, and made what is probably the first horror movie, *The Devil's Castle*, in 1896. Soon other French filmmakers, Leon Gaumont, and Charles and Emile Pathe among them, appeared on the scene. Meanwhile, other countries began developing their own movie industries. In the United States, Edison developed a projector in 1896. In 1903, Edwin S. Porter made the first American hit film, *The Great Train Robbery*. As independent moviemakers headed west, to the land of feature film production, Hollywood was born. The first sound film, *The Jazz Singer*, was released in 1927.

"FY Infopages" provide information on Louis Daguerre, Thomas Edison, Albert Dreyfus, Florence Lawrence (widely considered the first movie star), and the Academy Awards. Captioned black-and-white and color photo illustrations, a chronology, a Timeline of Discovery, and chapter notes are included. The use of purple and aqua pages results in an attractive and lively format. The book is an excellent source of basic information.

Glossary: Yes
Bibliography: Yes, of young adult books, works consulted, and
    Internet sites
Index: Yes
Level: Intermediate New Readers

Wilkes, Angela. *Best Book of Ballet*. Boston: Kingfisher, 2000.

Pages: 32
Series: —

Wilkes very briefly introduces the world of ballet. In just a few pages, she defines it; discusses famous ballets; and touches on learning to dance, what to wear, the basic positions, the learning process (from the classroom to the stage), creating a ballet, behind the scenes activity, costume and makeup, and the performance. The reader is guided through the different aspects of both classical and modern ballet. In addition, how dancers use mime and gesture to tell a story is explained.

The large print, simple language, and some illustrations identify the book as one for children. With this in mind, it is a useful title for adults seeking a source for quick answers on the subject.

Glossary: Yes
Bibliography: No
Index: Yes
Level: Beginning New Readers

❉ Biography ❉

Altman, Susan R. *Extraordinary Black Americans from Colonial to Contemporary Times.* Danbury, CT: Scholastic, 1992.

Pages: 208
Series: Extraordinary People

This well-written collection of short biographies provides an overview of the struggles and hardships black Americans had to endure in their quest for freedom and equality while illuminating the individual personalities of the famous and lesser-known biographies. Their philosophies, dedication to their causes, achievements, contributions to the development of American culture, society, and government, and, for many, their fates, are highlighted in the stories of the lives of such extraordinary figures as Crispus Attucks, Phillis Wheatley, Joseph Cinque, Dred Scott, Harriet Tubman, Frederick Douglass, Sojourner Truth, P.B.S. Pinchback, Booker T. Washington, Jan Ernst Matzeliger, Lewis Howard Latimer, Scott Joplin, Elijah McCoy, W.E.B. DuBois, William Christopher Handy. Paul Robeson, Marian Anderson, Ralph Bunche, Wilma Rudolph, Rosa Parks, James Baldwin, Thurgood Marshall, Malcolm X, Roy Wilkins, Toni Morrison, Guion Stewart Bluford, Martin Luther King, Jr., and Jesse Jackson. The text is augmented with accounts of slave uprisings, the black Seminoles, the underground railroad, the issuing of the Emanciption Proclamation, black Civil War soldiers, Reconstruction, 1960s sit-ins and freedom rides, the 1963 march on Washington, and the Black Power Movement. The book is enhanced by black-and-white illustrations, memorable quotations, and the text of the Emancipation Proclamation, the Reconstruction amendments to the U.S. Constitution, Elizabeth Eckford's account of day one at Central High School in Little Rock, Arkansas, Martin Luther King Jr.'s "Letter from Birmingham Jail," and his "I Have a Dream" speech. This title is well researched and written in a straightforward style.

Glossary: No
Bibliography: Yes
Index: Yes
Level: Advanced New Readers

Archer, Jules. *They Had a Dream: The Civil Rights Struggle from Frederick Douglass to Marcus Garvey to Martin Luther King, Jr. and Malcolm X.* Madison, WI: Turtleback, 1996.

Pages: 258
Series: Epoch Biographies

The manifestations of racism and bigotry and the fight for freedom and equal rights, from past to future means of destroying racial barriers, are detailed in two historical essays. Four men, Frederick Douglass, Marcus Garvey, Martin Luther King, Jr., and Malcolm X, were central to this equal rights struggle. Douglass was a powerful figure in the abolitionist movement; Garvey was the creator of black pride demonstrations and the leader of the "back to Africa" movement; King sought equal rights through nonviolent demonstrations and integration; and Malcolm X believed in racial separation and violent confrontation. The childhood influences on their lives, important adult life events, and achievements of these men are traced. Archer's compelling writing and rich information on racism, and political strife, defeat, intrigue, and hope, make this book an excellent resource.

Glossary: No
Bibliography: Yes
Index: Yes
Level: Advanced New Readers

Brown, Jordan D. *Robo World: The Story of Robot Designer Cynthia Breazeal.* Washington, DC: Joseph Henry Press, 2005.

Pages: 108
Series: Women's Adventures in Science

Brown profiles the life of Cynthia Breazeal, a roboticist who is presently the director of the Robotic Life Group at MIT's Media Lab. He tells of her early years as a curious and active child, her school years from grade school to graduate school—earning her doctor of science degree at MIT. Early in her career, Breazeal worked at Warner Brothers as a consultant for the marketing campaign for the film *AI: Artificial Intelligence* and then returned to MIT. The descriptions of her robot projects, two of which are Kismet, an emotionally intelligent robot, and Leonardo, an almost human robot because of the way it interacts with people, are clearly described, fascinating achievements. Breazeal's aim has been to create sociable robots that would exist to benefit people.

The book is well written and enhanced with photos from the scientist's personal album, as well as highlighted boxes with related information on Walt Disney's creations, a recipe for a robot, and putting a human face on robotics. There is a time line of Breazeal's life and a metric conversion chart. The author brings alive a vital young woman with a future of achievements yet to be realized. This book will interest anyone intrigued by robots and the people behind them.

Glossary: Yes
Bibliography: Yes, of books and Web sites
Index: Yes
Level: Intermediate–Advanced New Readers

Collier, Bruce and James MacLachlan. *Charles Babbage and the Engines of Perfection.* New York: Oxford University Press, 1999; softcover paperback reprint, Collingdale, PA: DIANE Publishing, 2006.

Pages: 128
Series: —

The authors blend the story of Babbage's personal life with a discussion of the man as mathematician and inventor of the Difference Machine and the Analytical Engine. Babbage designed these early calculating machines as he searched for a way to automatically calculate long tables of numbers. Although the Analytical Engine represented the concept of computer programming, Collier and MacLachlan point out that his designs were not fully implemented and had no impact on the later engineering design of the computer. Babbage has a place in history as a pioneer of the computer age—its "intellectual and spiritual ancestor." The discussions of the designs and functions of his machines are detailed and rather involved. The authors capture Babbage's personality as they trace his life from his childhood fascination with toys to his relationships with his father, wife, children, friends, and British scientific societies.

Black-and-white diagrams, photo reproductions with informative captions, and two-page sidebars on logarithms, differences in sequences of numbers, and the operation of the Jacquard Loom enhance the text. A chronology is included. This book is an excellent reference source sophisticated enough for adult readers.

Glossary: No
Bibliography: Yes, of books, museums and websites
Index: Yes
Level: Advanced New Readers

Cox, Clinton. *African American Healers.* New York: John Wiley, 2000.

Pages: 164
Series: Black Star Biography

This fascinating collection of short biographies of African-American doctors, nurses, and scientists, covers the periods from colonial America to the present. The book is divided into four parts: The Early Years, The Civil War Years and Reconstruction, Into The New Century, and Modern Times. Among the people highlighted are James Durham, who was born into slavery in 1762 and discovered an effective method for treating diptheria; Daniel Hale Williams (1856–1931), in 1893 the first to successfully perform heart surgery; Benjamin Solomon Carson (born 1951) the first to successfully separate Siamese twins joined at the back of the head; Dr. Charles Richard Drew (1904–1950), a pioneer, during World War II, in the development of blood plasma processing; and Dr. David Satcher (born 1941), appointed Surgeon General in 1998 by President Clinton. A number of notable women nurses and doctors are also listed, such as Susie King Taylor (1848–1912), Civil War nurse; Justina Laurena Ford (1871–1952), the first black female physician in the Rocky Mountains region of the United States; and Dr. Joycelyn Elders (born 1933), appointed Surgeon General in 1993.

Definitions of medical terms are scattered throughout the text. Fact boxes with further relevant information related to the biographies follow the entries. The book also includes a chronology and notes. This book is a well-written memorable reference source.

Glossary: No, but definitions within the text
Bibliography: Yes, of books, periodicals, and newspapers
Index: Yes
Level: Intermediate–Advanced New Readers

Freedman, Russell. *Franklin Delano Roosevelt.* Minneapolis: Sagebrush, 1990.

Pages: 200
Series: —

This excellent biography of Franklin Roosevelt begins with a brief overview of the major events in the life of the most controversial American president since Abraham Lincoln. The only president to serve 12 years in office, he led the country through the Great Depression and World War II. Roosevelt's many achievements are emphasized, including the expansion of the federal government; creation of unemployment insurance, social security, bank deposit insurance, minimum wage, maximum work hours, the federal welfare system, and the United Nations; and regulation of the stock market. A well-written text and many historic photographs bring the man and his times to life.

Glossary: No
Bibliography: Yes, a short chapter suggesting a few of the many
 books written about Roosevelt
Index: Yes, with page references to illustrations in italics
Level: Advanced New Readers

Freedman, Russell. *Lincoln: A Photobiography.* New York:
Clarion, 1989.

Pages: 160
Series: —

This well-researched text, combined with historic pictures of Lincoln,
his family, some famous contemporaries, Civil War battlefields, and
more, provides an intimate portrait of Lincoln. The real Lincoln is
brought to life through the recounting of his beliefs and his struggles with the difficult issues of the times. Each chapter is enhanced
with quotations that further define Honest Abe's greatness, and a
section of quotations from his letters and speeches, including
precise source information, follows the text. Historic sites located in
Kentucky, Illinois, and Washington, DC, are listed.

Glossary: No
Bibliography: Yes, of books about Lincoln
Index: Yes, with page references to illustrations in italics
Level: Advanced New Readers

Haskins, Jim. *Black Eagles: African Americans in Aviation.*
Madison, WI: Turtleback, 1997.

Pages: 196
Series: —

The emergence of black aviators and aviation communities began in
Los Angeles in the 1920s and in Chicago in the 1930s. Underlying the
passion for flying was the belief that gaining racial equality in the sky
would lead to the same on the ground. Surprisingly, a number of
famous black aviators were women, such as Marie Dickerson Coker,

who was responsible for the founding of the first Los Angeles all-black aero club, and Bessie Coleman, the first African American to be licensed as a pilot. Other notable aviators include James Herman Banning, the first black pilot to register for a license when the U.S Department of Commerce established aviation licensing laws in 1926; William J. Powell, author of the 1934 book *Black Wings* and the 1935 film *Unemployment, the Negro and Aviation*; Herbert Fauntleroy Julian, who made a successful parachute jump in April 1923 onto 139th Street in New York City's Harlem to call attention to African Americans in aviation; the World War II Tuskegee airmen who successfully influenced the decision to desegregate the military; Colonel Guion Bluford, the first black astronaut in space; and Mae C. Jemison, the first African-American woman in space.

The text is straightforward and filled with historical facts from the early years to the space age. Excellent photographic reproductions accompany the text. This aspect of the African-American struggle against discrimination is well presented and worthwhile reading.

Glossary: No
Bibliography: Yes, of books and periodical articles
Index: Yes
Level: Intermediate New Readers

Keenan, Sheila. *Scholastic Book of Outstanding Americans: Profiles of More Than 450 Famous and Infamous Figures in U.S. History.* New York: Scholastic, 2003.

Pages: 256
Series: —

In her introduction, Keenan states that this book is about more than 450 people who shaped, shook up, challenged, or changed American culture. They are outstanding in the sense of fame, but not necessarily upright—for example, Joseph McCarthy, Benedict Arnold, and Al Capone. The book includes sports figures, comedians, actors, first ladies, presidents, politicians, writers, scientists, religious leaders, musicians, composers, educators, doctors, inventors, rogues, and more and reveals how they influenced American life, culture, and history.

Each short entry identifies the person's vocation and includes birth and death dates and a photo illustration. Relevant quotes appear on most pages. This is an intriguing book for browsing and useful as a ready-reference source.

Glossary: Yes
Bibliography: Yes, of books and Web sites
Index: Yes
Level: Advanced New Readers

Krull, Kathleen. *Lives of the Artists: Masterpieces, Messes (and What the Neighbors Thought).* Illustrated by Kathryn Hewitt. San Diego: Harcourt Children's Books, 1995.

Pages: 96
Series: Lives of . . .

Before arriving at the title page, the reader learns that St. Luke is the patron saint of artists, as stated in the caption under a delightful full-page cartoon-like picture of him. The lives of 20 artists—Leonardo da Vinci, Michelangelo Buonarroti, Peter Bruegel, Sofonisba Anguissola, Rembrandt van Rijn, Katsushika Hokusai, Mary Cassatt, Vincent van Gogh, Kathe Kollwitz, Henri Matisse, Pablo Picasso, Marc Chagall, Marcel Duchamp, Georgia O'Keeffe, William H. Johnson, Salvador Dali, Isamu Noguchi, Diego Rivera, Frieda Kahlo, and Andy Warhol— are examined from the point of view of what their neighbors might have endured due to their rather noticeable, somewhat unusual lifestyles. Each piece is preceded by an informative cartoon and basic biographical data. An "Artworks" section, giving brief background information on some paintings, follows the short, lighthearted stories of the lives, times, and pecadillos of each artist.

Glossary: Yes, of artistic terms
Bibliography: Yes
Index: Yes, of artists
Level: Intermediate–Advanced New Readers

Krull, Kathleen. *Lives of Extraordinary Women: Rulers, Rebels (and What the Neighbors Thought).* Illustrated by Kathryn Hewitt. New York: Harcourt, 2000.

Pages: 95
Series: Lives of . . .

Athena, Greek goddess of handicraft, war, and wisdom (pictured opposite the title page) most definitely influenced the choice of the 20 women for this book. These women dared to enter politics and, in some cases, became heads of state. Summaries of heroic and tragic events in the lives of Cleopatra, Eleanor of Aquitaine, Joan of Arc, Isabella I, Elizabeth I, Nzingha (West African queen), Catherine the Great, Marie Antoinette, Victoria, Harriet Tubman, Tz'u-Hsi (empress of China), Gertrude Bell (the uncrowned queen of Iraq), Jeanette Rankin (first Congresswoman), Eleanor Roosevelt, Golda Meir, Indira Gandhi, Eva Peron, Wilma Mankiller (American Indian leader), Aung San Suu Kyi (Burmese revolutionary leader), and Rigoberta Menchu (Guatamalan leader). The short biographical pieces reveal each woman's eccentricities, along with facts about their lives as children, how they lived as adults, what they wore and ate, and their work. Birth and death dates and a brief statement of who they were and what they are famous for precedes each entry. The "Ever After" section that follows the text provides additional information. Hewitt's humorous illustrations definitely add to the appeal of this unique title.

Glossary: No
Bibliography: Yes
Index: No, but the table of contents does the job
Level: Intermediate–Advanced New Readers

Krull, Kathleen. *Lives of the Musicians: Good Times, Bad Times (and What the Neighbors Thought).* Illustrated by Kathryn Hewitt. Minneapolis: Sagebrush, 2002.

Pages: 96
Series: Lives of . . .

Under the watchful eye of Saint Cecilia (pictured opposite the title page), protector of musicians, are succinctly told the stories of the lives of Antonio Vivaldi, Johann Sebastian Bach, Wolfgang Amadeus Mozart, Ludwig van Beethoven, Frederic Chopin, Giuseppe Verdi, Clara Schumann, Stephen Foster, Johannes Brahms, Peter Ilich Tchaikovsky, William Gilbert and Arthur Sullivan, Erik Satie, Scott Joplin, Charles Ives, Igor Stravinsky, Nadia Boulanger, Sergei Prokofiev, George Gershwin, and Woody Guthrie. The humorous, and often rather sad, eccentricities of each musical talent, along with facts about their lives as children, what they wore and ate, and how they lived, are revealed from the viewpoint of observing neighbors. The short biographical pieces are filled with many facts not readily available in the usual encyclopedias of music and musicians. The birth and death dates and a brief summary of the musician's life introduces each entry, and the "Musical Notes" section that follows the text provides additional information. The humorous approach makes this an extremely appealing title.

Glossary: Yes, of musical terms
Bibliography: Yes, of books and recordings
Index: Yes, of composers
Level: Intermediate–Advanced New Readers

Krull, Kathleen. *Lives of the Writers: Comedies, Tragedies (and What the Neighbors Thought).* Illustrated by Kathryn Hewitt. San Diego: Harcourt Children's Books, 1994.

Pages: 96
Series: Lives of . . .

The reader learns at the very beginning that Calliope and Thalia, pictured in a cartoon illustration, are the goddesses of literary inspiration. Summaries of the comedic or tragic events that inspired the creativity and writing successes of Murasaki Shikibu, Miguel de Cervantes, William Shakespeare, Jane Austen, Hans Christian Andersen, Edgar Allen Poe, Charles Dickens, Charlotte and Emily Bronte, Emily Dickinson, Louisa May Alcott, Mark Twain, Frances Hodgson Burnett, Robert Louis Stevenson, Jack London, Carl Sandburg, E.B. White,

Zora Neale Hurston, Langston Hughes, and Isaac Bashevis Singer are placed between brief biographical data and a "Bookmarks" section that presents additional information on each writer's life and works. Aided by Hewitt's effective and informative cartoons, the book provides an enjoyable look at some writers who were either quiet or noisy neighbors. It is a good source of significant and interesting information.

Glossary: Yes, of literary terms
Bibliography: Yes
Index: Yes, of writers
Level: Intermediate–Advanced New Readers

Parker, Steve. *Aristotle and Scientific Thought.* New York: Chelsea House, 1995.

Pages: 32
Series: —

The ancient Greeks considered science to be part of philosophy, seeking the truth, the essence of thinking, and the nature of knowledge and existence. To better illuminate Aristotle's life and works, the author begins with a very brief history of ancient Greece and Greek philosophers. Then, Aristotle's interest in nature, biology, and anatomy, his study under Plato at Athens, the founding of his own school, his final years, his achievements, and his influence on later scientists are clearly discussed. Additional information on related topics, such as science before the Greeks, Greek medicine, the philosophies of Socrates and Plato, Aristotle's theory of four elements, and how his theory of anatomy evolved over the centuries, enhance the text. A two-page chart of the world in Aristotle's time shows developments in the fields of science, exploration, politics, and the arts. The illustrations and informative captions further complement the text. There is a surprising amount of detail in this easy-to-understand presentation of a complex subject.

Glossary: Yes
Bibliography: No
Index: Yes
Level: Beginning New Readers

Pinkney, Andrea Davis. *Let It Shine: Stories of Black Women Freedom Fighters.* Illustrated by Stephen Alcorn. New York: Gulliver Books, 2000.

Pages: 108
Series: —

Pinkney focuses on ten women who together outline the history of the fight for civil rights from the eighteenth century to the present. These women fought for the freedom to choose and to speak out in newspapers and television and freedom from oppression and sexism—in short, equal rights. Brief chapters relate the mark each woman made in American history, beginning with Sojourner Truth and including Biddy Mason, Harriet Tubman, Ida B. Wells-Bornett, Mary McLeod Bethune, Ella Josephine Baker, Dorothy Irene Height, Rosa Parks, Fanny Lou Hamer, and Shirley Chisholm. Their primary goal, the achievement of civil rights, was so hard fought that it led to a congresswoman actually running for president.

The text, together with the artwork, presents a meaningful exploration of the subject. An outstanding reading experience, the book suits both adults and children.

Glossary: No
Bibliography: Yes, of general historical titles and biographies of the
    freedom fighters
Index: No
Level: Intermediate–Advanced New Reader

Ring, Elizabeth. *Rachel Carson: Caring for the Earth.*
Minneapolis: Lerner, 1992.

Pages: 48
Series: Gateway Greens

This brief, simply written biography tells the story of Rachel Carson's life: her childhood, her mother's influence on her youthful fascination with nature, and her heroic efforts to make people aware of the need to protect the environment. Ring touches on the message of

Carson's books: *Under the Sea Wind, The Sea Around Us, The Edge of the Sea, Silent Spring,* and *A Sense of Wonder.* Finally, the author speculates on what Carson's reaction would be to today's world environmental groups, the controls placed on toxic waste and chemicals that pollute the earth and atmosphere, and recycling efforts. Photographs and a chronology enhance the text. This easy-to-read biography of a prominent marine biologist and pioneer in the environmental movement is a good choice for adult beginning readers.

Glossary: No
Bibliography: Yes
Index: Yes
Level: Beginning New Readers

Scheller, William. *The World's Greatest Explorers.* Foreword by Robert D. Ballard. Minneapolis: Oliver, 1992.

Pages: 160
Series: Profiles

A concise discussion of reasons people leave home to explore the earth, this book introduces some famous explorers who mapped out the geography of the world and answered many questions about climate, resources, and topography. The lives, travels, and discoveries of Muhammad ibn Batuta, Vasco da Gama, James Cook, Samuel de Champlain, Jacques Marquette, Alexander Mackenzie, Meriwether Lewis and William Clark, John Charles Fremont, Robert Perry and Matthew Henson, and Roald Amundsen are summarized in chapters less than 20 pages long. Quite a bit of material is packed into this text. Captioned black-and-white pictures of the explorers and scenes related to their travels provide additional information. Maps of exploration and expedition routes are clearly drawn and easily understood. A handy chronology of explorers and world events is included. The book contains much worthwhile biographical and historical data.

Glossary: No
Bibliography: Yes

Index: Yes
Level: Intermediate–Advanced New Readers

Shapiro, Marc. *J.K. Rowling: The Wizard Behind Harry Potter.*
New York: St. Martins Griffin, 2004.

Pages: 228
Series: —

The story behind J.K. Rowling's rise to fame answers burning questions concerning Harry Potter's creator. Shapiro traces her life from child to single mother, reveals where the Potter idea came from, how fame changed Rowling, where the name "Harry Potter" originated, and what her rules about writing are. A few black-and-white photographs are included. This unauthorized biography is a quick and easy read.

Glossary: No
Bibliography: No—sources are listed at the front of the book
Index: No
Level: Beginning New Readers

Sproule, Anna. *James Watt: Master of the Steam Engine.*
Woodbridge, CT: Blackbirch, 2001.

Pages: 64
Series: Giants of Science

This is a concise biography of an eighteenth-century Scottish inventor and engineer who, from childhood on, was fascinated by things mechanical. He graduated from repairing surveying instruments to making musical instruments, to improving the Newcomer pump, to perfecting the steam engine. Sproule intertwines Watt's story with the history of the Industrial Revolution. The clear narrative is enhanced by detailed color and black-and-white illustrations. A time line is included. Authoritative, nicely formatted, and written in clear, mature language, this title serves as a good basic resource.

Glossary: Yes
Bibliography: Yes, of three titles and a Web site

Index: Yes
Level: Beginning New Reader

Stanley, Diane. *Leonardo da Vinci.* New York: HarperCollins, 2000.

Pages: 48
Series: —

In this comprehensive biography of Leonardo da Vinci, pages of well-written descriptive text alternate with full-page paintings that illustrate significant scenes from his life and work. Examples of drawings from Leonardo's notebooks appear at the top of each page of text, which is also adorned with a border design adopted from da Vinci's own designs. The book is rich with facts about the artist's life, his art, and other achievements (music, scientific discoveries, designs, and descriptions of inventions) as revealed in his note-books—all the products of a phenomenal mind. Any reader is bound to be captivated by this remarkable book.

Glossary: No, but a pronunciation guide appears on the verso of
    the title page
Bibliography: Yes, of adult titles and books recommended for
    younger readers
Index: No
Level: Beginning–Intermediate New Readers

Weidhorn, Manfred. *Jackie Robinson.* New York: Atheneum, 1993.

Pages: 207
Series: —

The story of Jackie Robinson's life includes his birth and early expe-riences with racial prejudice to the emergence of his athletic talent; his role as the first African American to play major league baseball; the difficulties of overcoming racial discrimination despite his record-breaking baseball career; his induction into the Baseball

Hall of Fame in July 1962; his retirement from the game; his post-baseball career in business and politics; and his active role as spokesman for the Civil Rights movement. A few photographs are included. An engaging chronicle of the man who, with Branch Rickey, the general manager of the Brooklyn Dodgers, broke the tradition of barring black baseball players from major league teams, the book reveals not only the life of an outstanding athlete, but a man of strength, intelligence, and extraordinary determination.

Glossary: No
Bibliography: Yes, an annotated list of comprehensive, scholarly
    books
Index: Yes
Level: Advanced New Readers

Computer Technology

Berry, Charles W. and William H. Hawn. *Computer and Internet Dictionary for Ages 9–99.* Hauppauge, NY: Barron's, 2000.

Pages: 230
Series: —

A short introduction is followed by clear instructions on how to use the book, a one-and-one-half page history of computers, a concise explanation of the Internet, a page showing both PC and MacIntosh keyboard layouts, and definitions of symbols and numbers used in the book. The body of the book contains over 800 definitions of computer and Internet terms. They are defined in nontechnical language and accompanied by examples explaining key concepts, cross-references, and practical tips. Color cartoon illustrations clarify definitions, particularly for readers with limited computer literacy. Back matter includes a table of abbrievations used in e-mail, chat and Usenet; a table of binary and hexidecimal numbers from 0 to 255; country codes and suffixes used in e-mail addresses; a table of metric prefixes, thickness measurements, or point sizes used in graphics; word processing; and a table of font types. Some games, followed by the answers to them, encourages writing in the book—a disadvantage for libraries considering acquiring it. This is a handy source for quick answers for those in need of a user-friendly dictionary of terms and concepts.

Glossary: No
Bibliography: Yes, of suggested readings
Index: No
Level: Beginning–Advanced New Readers

Claybourne, Anna. *Computer Dictionary for Beginners.*
Minneapolis: Sagebrush, 2001.

Pages: 64
Series: —

What does the inside of a computer mouse look like, and how does it work? What is a "bus"? What is a "virtual relationship"? What do PCMCIA and EFTPOS stand for? Does one really go "logging" on a computer?

Answers to all these questions and many more can be found in this remarkably comprehensive revised and updated book. It is more than a dictionary. It has chapters that cover various computer-related subjects such as essential computer words, input and output devices, the processing unit, types of computers, printers, peripherals, memory and storage, software, programming, computer problems and solutions, living with computers, the Internet, and the history of computers. The clear, concise definitions and explanations are beautifully complemented by captioned and labeled color pictures and diagrams. There are a number of ways to locate data, as the section on using the dictionary explains. With the table of contents, the reader can locate a particular topic, such as sound and music software. Bold typeface highlights words that are defined or explained. Italic typeface indicates words that are discussed in more detail on another page, and these pages are footnoted with asterisks. The glossaries and index provide further finding tools. This is a dictionary for the computer novice, the technophobe, and the computer-knowledgeable person looking for a quick reference tool.

Glossary: Yes
Bibliography: No
Index: Yes
Level: Beginning–Intermediate New Reader

Cochrane, Kerry. *Internet.* Danbury, CT: Franklin Watts, 1995.

Pages: 64
Series: A First Book

Quite a number of librarians recommend this book as a good, brief history of the Internet, beginning with its development in the late 1960s as a U.S. Department of Defense project. It clearly explains how the Internet works. It briefly discusses address components and the six domains (com = commercial organization, edu = educational site, etc.) that appear at the end of an Internet address, identifies the Internet's major functions, and explains how to find information on the Internet. The last chapter is clearly meant for children who are ready to start exploring the Internet. It illustrates some sites of interest to young people. This chapter, plus the reference to kids on the back cover of the book, should not discourage adult Internet novices from using it as a brief introduction to a complex system. Helpful reproductions of sample screens serve to clarify the text.

Glossary: Yes
Bibliography: No
Index: Yes
Level: Beginning New Readers

Darling, David. *Computers of the Future: Intelligent Machines and Virtual Reality.* Parsippany, NJ: Silver Burdett, 1995.

Pages: 72
Series: Beyond Two Thousand

This brief, well-illustrated book covers the evolution of computers from the abacus to a humanoid robot. Darling describes the role computers play in everyday life and highlights what is good about computers (e.g., speed and efficiency, rapid access to a vast body of information, ability to accomplish tasks that would be dangerous for humans) as well as some negatives, including invasion of privacy, hacker-altered and deleted records, viruses that destroy data and cause system failure, faulty chips causing data errors, proliferation of junk information, and the danger of long periods of time spent in the imaginary world of virtual reality. Carefully captioned full-color photos and highlighted boxes of related facts extend the information provided in the text.

Glossary: Yes
Bibliography: Yes
Index: Yes
Level: Beginning–Intermediate New Readers

Goranson, Christopher D. *Everything You Need to Know About Misinformation on the Internet.* New York: Rosen, 2002.

Pages: 64
Series: Need to Know Library

The Internet provides fast communication and a venue to promote and sell just about anything—much legitimate, some not—and nearly every subject can be researched on countless sites. Of course, there is a caveat: the information may not be accurate, and sites may not be authoritative or up to date.

Goranson concisely reviews the question of Internet regulation, listing the top ten "dot-cons," that is, auction frauds, Internet service provider scams, pyramid scams, and travel/vacation frauds. He discusses how to stay safe in chat rooms and news groups and on e-mail, how to check facts and evaluate informational Web pages, and how to judge e-commerce sites. Goranson includes lists of national fraud information centers; five things to look for when shopping online; online services for investigating Web sites before buying on the Internet; the Federal Trade Commission's suggestions to help Internet users protect themselves from business-related fraud.

The book is nicely formatted with bulleted lists highlighted in blue, captioned illustrations, and photographs. It is appropriate for adults, teens, and older children looking for a handy guide to intelligent use of the Internet.

Glossary: Yes
Bibliography: Yes, of books for adults, organizations, and Web
    sites
Index: Yes
Level: Beginning–Intermediate Reading Levels

Packard, Mary. *High-Tech Inventions.* New York: Children's Press, 2004.

Pages: 48
Series: True Tales

Various hi-tech inventions are mentioned, beginning with ENIAC (the first general-purpose electronic computer), in the single-page introduction. Then the reader is invited to read the stories behind the inventions and perhaps become inspired to invent as well. The first chapter is a brief narrative about Jack Kilby and Robert Noyce, two scientists who invented the same thing in 1958—the integrated circuit, with a look at ENIAC (1945, University of Pennsylvania) and its vacuum tubes, the invention of the transistor, and the shrinking of computer size to those of today—desk, lap, and palm size. Chapter 2 talks about Professor Isao Shimoyama, University of Tokyo, and his Robo-roach, a live cockroach controlled by remote control, and the precursor, wireless technology. Charles Gibson's Segway HT (Human Transporter), developed as an answer to the air pollution problem that made a small media splash a few years ago (date not given in the text) is discussed in Chapter 3. The final chapter looks at Michael Moshier's personal flying machine, introduced in 2001.

A generous number of photo illustrations are included on almost every page. The large print, small size, and simple language identify this title as a children's book. It is included because it might suit the older reader with a limited command of English and an interest in the history of computers. It could thus serve as a lead-in to the subject.

Glossary: Yes
Bibliography: Yes, of books and Web sites
Index: Yes
Level: Beginning New Readers

Parks, Peggy J. *The Internet.* Farmington Hills, MI: Gale, 2004.

Pages: 48
Series: KidHaven Science Library

This book is a clear, concise history of the development of the Internet, from its beginnings in the 1960s to today's enormous network of networks, the World Wide Web, and the simplification of searching. In 1993, two years after the Web was released to the public, there were 130 Web sites. By 2002, the number of sites had grown to 600 million. The author touches on how the Internet is used and it's effect on society—commerce, education, literacy, communication, and net crime. Illustrations include photographs, a map of the birth of the Internet, a graph showing the growth of the Internet, and a chart demonstrating how the Internet works, and the chapters have notes. This title offers a simple explanation of a subject daunting to many adults, if one can get past the "Kid" in Kidhaven (the series name).

Glossary: Yes
Bibliography: Yes, of books, periodicals, Internet sources, and Web
    sites
Index: Yes
Level: Beginning New Readers

Rothman, Kevin F. *Coping with Dangers on the Internet: Staying Safe On-Line.* New York: Rosen, 2001.

Pages: 121
Series: —

Rothman provides general safety guidelines for sending and receiving e-mail; surfing the World Wide Web; using chat rooms, newsgroups, and mailing lists; and publishing on the Web. He states that the best defense against Internet dangers is to understand what the Internet is and how it works. The author describes the Internet infrastructure, ways to connect to it (cable, DSL, cell phone, etc.), and Internet areas—Web sites, chat rooms, instant messaging, newsgroups, mailing lists, and more.

Sound advice is given about choosing a password—changing it often and not giving it out; using credit cards on reputable service sites; using an antivirus program and firewall; backing up data; not responding to questionable e-mails; not believing everything you read, and more. There are lists of Web sites to avoid organizations and Web sites to go to for help and information about chat rooms, newsgroups, auctions, and copyright and trademark issues. If adults can ignore the references to asking parents, they will find this title an easy-to-read, practical guide to staying safe online.

Glossary: Yes
Bibliography: Yes
Index: Yes
Level: Beginning–Intermediate New Readers

Sherman, Josepha. *The History of the Internet.* New York: Franklin Watts, 2003.

Pages: 64
Series: Watts Library

Sherman explores the history of the Internet—how it was developed, the people involved in its origins, how it was improved, and its future capabilities. Its evolution is traced from the Department of Defense design of ARPANET (the first electronic network) to Ray Tomlinson's addition of the @ sign to improve e-mail addresses (1971), the development of various organizers (filing systems like GOPHER, ARCHIE, VERONICA), and on to the World Wide Web— commercial online service providers (the first being Compuserve, then AOL) and Web browsers (Netscape Navigator, 1994; Microsoft Internet Explorer, 1998) and Web-based research engines, such as Alta Vista (1995), Excite.com (1995), LYCOS.com, HotBot.com, Google.com, and Yahoo.com (1995–1998). Sherman points out that today's Internet has an increasing problem of security and privacy— with identity theft a major issue. She notes its many uses, from medical consultations to communication in space, and that there will be more as the Internet grows. There are ample photo illustrations, some useful diagrams, and highlighted fact boxes. The book provides a quick history for those wanting just the essentials.

Glossary: Yes
Bibliography: Yes, of books, organizations, and online sites

Index: Yes
Level: Beginning–Intermediate New Readers

Sherman, Josepha. *The History of the Personal Computer.* New York: Franklin Watts, 2003.

Pages: 64
Series: Watts Library

Sherman takes readers on a trip down personal computer memory lane. She traces its development from the dawn of computers in 1642 through Joseph Marie Jacquard and his loom; Charles Babbage and the analytical engine; Herman Hollerith, who encoded data by punching cards with a series of holes; and on to ENIAC, UNIVAC in the 1940s, the IBM 650 (the first mass-produced computer in the 1950s), Jobs' and Wozinac's Apple II in 1977, the 1980s Intel computer chip, Microsoft DOS, Bill Gates' versions of Windows, to today's notebooks. There is a section on the future of the computer and a time line. Words in boldface within the text are defined in the glossary. Numerous illustrations and fact boxes add to the content. This will interest those seeking a brief overview of the subject as well as a concise discussion of the scientists who contributed to the development of personal computers.

Glossary: Yes.
Bibliography: Yes, of books, organizations, and Web sites
Index: Yes, with numbers in italics indicating illustrations
Level: Beginning–Intermediate New Readers

Williams, Brian. *Computers.* Chicago: Heinemann, 2002.

Pages: 48
Series: Great Inventions

In this short history, double-page chapters touch on the technology and inventions related to computers: the abacus, slide rule, calculator, punched card, Babbage's computer, census counter, electronic tube, electronic computer, colossus, transistor, floppy disk, robots, integrated circuits, virtual reality, electronic calculator, bar code, personal computer, CD-ROM, Internet, and e-books. The book is illustrated with black-and-white and color photographs, graphs, and a key date chart that runs through it. Sidebars define terms and provide brief biographical information about inventors. A time line is included. This title provides a concise overview of the subject.

Glossary: Yes
Bibliography: Yes, of three books
Index: Yes
Level: Beginning–Intermediate New Readers

Worland, Gayle. *The Computer.* Mankato, MN: Capstone, 2004.

Pages: 32
Series: Fact Finders

In 1997, chess champion Garry Kasparov played chess with IBM's Deep Blue, programmed to look at 200 million possible chess moves per second. Deep Blue won. This event is described in the first chapter, "Man Versus Machine," and Worland asks if this was an indication of the future and whether computers might be more intelligent than people. She answers with a No—people make computers to make life easier. The author then backs up and presents a brief history of the computer, from the ancient abacus to the present personal computer. A brief explanation of binary digits is followed by a look at computers today—oddly with no mention of laptops—and how they are used. A time line follows the text (with an illustration of a surprisingly old laptop model). There is a page of "Fast Facts" and instructions on writing in binary code. Despite its simple language and large print, the book is appropriate for beginning adult students interested in the basics of the subject.

Glossary: Yes
Bibliography: Yes, of four books and a Web site
Index: Yes
Level: Beginning New Readers

✿ Cookbooks and Cookery ✿

Buller, Laura. *Food.* New York: DK, 2005.

Pages: 72
Series: Eyewitness

Short chapters with brief text, striking full-color photographs, and clear, concise captions make this title a good reference source. It is jam-packed with information on all aspects of food: the web of life, calories, food guide pyramid, choosing healthy foods, carbohydrates, fiber, good and bad fats, protein, minerals, healing foods, allergies and toxins, digestion and absorption, food and culture, attitudes toward food, crop staples, dairy foods, livestock, fish and seafood, the GM (genetically modified) debate, organic foods, and more. The final chapter looks at the question of how food will be provided to everyone on the planet without destroying the environment. Included are a list of amazing facts; questions and answers about food; record breakers, for example, largest box of chocolates, biggest food fight; and a time line of important events in food history.

Glossary: Yes
Bibliography: Yes, of Web sites and places to visit in the United States and Canada
Index: Yes
Level: Beginning–Intermediate New Readers

Burleigh, Robert. *Chocolate: Riches from the Rain Forest.* New York: Harry N. Abrams, 2002.

Pages: Unpaginated
Series: —

From hot chocolate to hot fudge sundaes, from chocolate cheesecake to chocolate candy bars, chocolate is by far the most beloved taste for many people. It is dark and bittersweet or light and creamy, smooth, heavenly, and mouthwatering—in short, indescribably luscious and unforgettable. Like most chocolate lovers, the author admits that he knew little about the long history of chocolate and less about how it is made. He turned to the researchers at Chicago's Field Museum for their knowledge and research recommendations. This impressive book is the result of Burleigh's efforts. He discusses the making of chocolate, from harvesting the seeds of the cacao tree to modern techniques, and traces the history of chocolate from the Olmecs, who first broke open the pods 3,000 years ago, to its popularity in Europe and America.

An amazing array of photo illustrations with informative captions enriches the text—printed on various shades of brown pages. Large-print subject headings make finding topics by flipping through the pages an easy process—a good substitute for the missing table of contents and index. The narrative flows as smoothly as melted chocolate and is as satisfying as a chocolate bonbon. This title is as much for adults as for children.

Glossary: Yes
Bibliography: Yes
Index: No
Level: Beginning–Intermediate New Readers

Chung, Okwha and Judy Monroe. *Cooking the Korean Way.*
Revised and expanded to include new low-fat and vegetarian recipes. Minneapolis: Lerner, 2003.

Pages: 72
Series: Easy Menu Ethnic Cookbooks

The book begins with an introduction to the geography and history of Korea, the foods that North and South Korea share, Korean holidays and festivals, and useful instructions on how to eat with chopsticks. There are guidelines on what to do before starting to cook: read the recipe through, know what ingredients to shop for, and follow basic safety rules. Also included is a list of cooking utensils, cooking terms, and definitions of special ingredients, such as Chinese cabbage, daikon radish, millet, tofu, and wonton skins. There is a page of tips for healthy and low-fat cooking and a table of metric conversions. The author explains the Korean table setup and menu—noting that there is little difference in what is served for breakfast, lunch, and dinner. Rice and kimchi (a pickle) are eaten at every meal. The recipe names appear in both English and Korean and are complemented by full-color, mouth-watering photographs. A map of Korea is also included.

This revised and expanded edition offers a generous number of tantalizing recipes, with step-by-step instructions. Even so, preparation will be difficult for less than seasoned cooks. This title should be of interest to adults, with or without a child assisting.

Other cookbooks in the series feature African, Australian, Caribbean, Chinese, French, German, Indian, Italian, Japanese, Lebanese, Mexican, and Polish cooking.

See NGUYEN, CHI AND JUDY MONROE for a related title in the same series.

Glossary: No
Bibliography: No
Index: Yes
Level: Intermediate New Readers

D'Amico, Joan and Karen Eich Drummond. *United States Cookbook: Fabulous Foods and Fascinating Facts from All 50 States.* New York: John Wiley, 2000.

Pages: 186
Series: —

This is a delicious introduction to the 50 states, including a brief history of each and its capital, animal, bird, insect, tree, and flower.

There are simple maps that show the locations of the capital and other major cities. A recipe from each state—Connecticut's Election Day Cake, Florida's Key Lime Pie, Nebraska's Reuben Sandwich, Montana's Cheyenne Butter Bread, Washington State's Baked Apples, to name a few—is included. Each is kid tested and easy to follow for a child or the worst adult cook. "Fun Food Facts" boxes offer some entertaining trivia, such as that Philadelphia is the birthplace of the ice cream soda and that much of the world's supply of horseradish comes from Illinois. The book begins with a section that defines various utensils and cooking skills. The safety rules, like getting an adult's permission before using the stove or oven, identify the book as one for kids. Despite the obvious kid features, the recipes are worthwhile for adults and great for learning how to cook (with or without kids in the kitchen) while expanding one's recipe repertoire.

A companion volume by the same authors, *The Coming to America Cookbook: Delicious Recipes and Fascinating Stories from America's Many Cultures* (New York: John Wiley, 2005: 192 pages) is a perfect fit for new Americans wanting to teach their children how to make traditional dishes and to learn about some of the recipes from other immigrants, including main and side dishes, vegetarian meals, and desserts. Eighteen countries are represented in the companion volume, including background information on how the country's climate, geography, culture, and history influences cooking and dining. The recipes are not necessarily for children only, because the ingredients are rather specialized and the techniques rather complicated.

Glossary: No, but some terms are defined in the text
Bibliography: No
Index: Yes
Level: Intermediate New Readers

Kalman, Bobbie and Ellen Brown. *The Colonial Cookbook.*
Illustrated by Barbara Bedell. New York: Crabtree, 2002.

Pages: 32
Series: Colonial People

Exactly who were the Colonial cooks? Women, daughters, men (cooks and bakers in taverns and on plantations), unmarried men and widowers, indentured servants, and slaves. The author describes the cooking fire and how it was used. A double-page section defines and illustrates the pots, pans, and utensils used in the Colonial kitchen. The big house, or plantation kitchen, is explained—followed by a look at different kinds of dependencies (small buildings) where foods were stored and prepared: the chicken coop, root cellar, smoke house, well house, and dairy. There are chapters on foods grown and raised, harvesting and processing for storage, preparation of food for the day, and the dinnertime meal. Safety tips, cooking terms, and some traditional recipes and leftovers recipes for supper are included in a double-page section. The final two double-page sections look at Native American foods and African-American cooking, including a recipe for each. Although the book is aimed at a young audience, an adult is required in the kitchen to prepare the recipes. The book is a short and simple introduction to the subject, particularly for adults just learning English and American history, and has appealing color illustrations.

Glossary: Yes
Bibliography: No
Index: Yes
Level: Beginning New Readers

Katzen, Mollie. *Honest Pretzels and 64 Other Amazing Recipes for Kids.* Berkeley, CA: Tricycle, 2004.

Pages: 192
Series: —

This fascinating title offers a substantial collection of vegetarian recipes for breakfast dishes, soups, salads and sandwiches for lunch and dinner, main and side dishes, desserts, baked goods, snacks, and drinks. Katzen's intent is for older kids to share the joys of the meal preparation experience with adult help, become familiar with and appreciate fresh fruit and vegetables, and aquire some cooking skills while using a bit of math, science, and logic and developing a sense of accomplishment. An introduction precedes each dish and includes some background information and safety tips. Lists of ingredients and necessary utensils accompany visual step-by-step numbered instructions and recommendations on when to ask an adult for help. Indeed, the virtues of cooking from scratch are evident for each dish—for example, those Honest Pretzels are certainly superior from store bought—with the added fun of making them in a variety of shapes. This enjoyable book has a nice upbeat flavor to it, enticing the reader to try out some (or even all) of the appetizing recipes, such as Eggflower Soup, Spunky Chili, Peanut Butter Doo-Dads, Made-in-the-Pan Chocolate Cake, Hip Bean Dip, and Purple Passion Power Shake. Entertaining quotations appear occasionally throughout the text.

Although designed for older children, adult help is necessary for each recipe. The word "Kids" in the subtitle should be disregarded, for this serves also as a book for adults who want to learn to cook but are challenged by boiling water and scrambling eggs.

Glossary: No
Bibliography: No
Index: Yes
Level: Intermediate–Advanced New Readers

Nguyen, Chi and Judy Monroe. *Cooking the Vietnamese Way: Includes New Low-Fat and Vegetarian Recipes.* Minneapolis: Lerner, 2003.

Pages: 72
Series: Easy Menu Ethnic Cookbooks

Here is an appetizing presentation of Vietnamese cuisine and recipes that are simple to understand and follow. An introduction, complete with a map of Vietnam that illustrates where various foodstuffs originate, offers a concise description of the land, traditions, holiday feasts, and information on Vietnamese foods in general. There is a handy list of cooking utensils, cooking terms, and ingredients and illustrated instructions on how to eat with chopsticks. A Vietnamese menu (in English and Vietnamese) of staples (rice and noodles, for example), salads, soups, and stir-fried, fried, grilled, braised, simmered, and steamed dishes includes a pronunciation guide. Recipes include lists of ingredients in boldface and are easy to follow, and the safety tips for cooks, metric conversion chart, and table of common measures and their equivalents are helpful. The pictures certainly do make one want to taste the food. This is an enjoyable title for the adult reader with a culinary bent.

Other cookbooks in the series feature African, Australian, Caribbean, Chinese, French, German, Indian, Italian, Japanese, Lebanese, Mexican, and Polish cooking.

See CHUNG, OKWHA AND JUDY MONROE for a related title of interest.

Glossary: No
Bibliography: No
Index: Yes
Level: Beginning–Intermediate New Readers

Nottridge, Rhoda. *Sugars.* Illustrated by John Yates. Minneapolis: Carolrhoda, 1993.

Pages: 32
Series: Food Facts

This quick and readable lesson on sugars informs the reader that too much sugar can be unhealthy even though it makes food taste good and is a source of quick energy. Different types of sugar are clearly defined: sucrose, or refined sugar derived from sugar cane or sugar beets; fructose, the primary sugar in honey and found in almost all fruits and many vegetables; glucose, also in fruits and vegetables and the sugar found in the blood; maltose, formed from grains and other starches; and lactose, present in milk and dairy products. The author briefly discusses sweetness and how plants make sugar, how sugar cane and sugar beets are grown (with a world map showing where each comes from), and how sugar is processed and refined. A concise history of sugar is followed by two short paragraphs on artificial sweeteners. A description of how honey is made precedes a recipe for a honey-yogurt topping, served with fruit salad or a dessert.

The large print, simple text, projects, and illustrations picturing children make the juvenile nature of the book obvious. However, some librarians recommend the book for quick reference use for adults because it contains easily accessible, useful facts on the subject.

Glossary: Yes, with words included appearing in boldface within the text
Bibliography: Yes, of secondary sources limited to three children's books
Index: Yes
Level: Beginning New Readers

Ventura, Piero et al. *Food: Its Evolution Through the Ages.*
Reprint. Collindale, PA: DIANE Publishing, 1998.

Pages: 64
Series: —

The evolution of food and the emergence of food science are traced from primitive times, when hunters caught their prey by using holes and cliffs as traps, to modern methods of breeding, cultivation, and food preservation. The text nicely summarizes the development of agriculture and includes a two-page discussion of the genetic engineering and cellular fusion processes that scientists are studying in order to create new and larger plants, such as the "pomato," which would produce tomatoes on the upper plant and potatoes as part of the root system. The author also touches on hybridization to increase plant productivity and resistance to disease. A section on the importance of including a variety of food types in the diet also lists the number of calories consumed during various activities (sleeping, walking, driving, swimming). Attractive illustrations and numerous highlighted boxes provide additional information and little-known facts. This is an absorbing history of civilization based on the human need for food to sustain health and prolong life.

Glossary: Yes
Bibliography: No
Index: No
Level: Intermediate New Readers

Wolfe, Robert. Vegetarian Cookery Around the World.
Minneapolis: Sagebrush, 1992.

Pages: 47
Series: —

Vegetarianism is clearly defined in the introduction, which includes a map depicting the parts of the world where it is the diet of choice for economic and/or religious reasons. The need for meat protein in the diet is discussed, and cooking utensils, cooking terms, and special ingredients are listed. A simple menu with an international flavor includes the ethnic names of the various foods, a pronunciation guide, and the countries of origin. The recipes for beverages, breads and staples, breakfast, lunch, dinner, and dessert are easy to follow. The ingredients are listed in boldface, and the illustrations are enticing. Cooking safety rules are included, as is a metric conversion chart and common measures and their equivalents. This book has an excellent format for beginning adult readers and novice ethnic cooks of any age.

Glossary: No
Bibliography: No
Index: Yes
Level: Beginning New Readers

✹ Cultural Mores ✹
and Institutions

Ashabranner, Brent. *Remembering Korea: The Korean War Veterans Memorial.* Photographed by Jennifer Ashabranner. Brookfield, CT: Twenty-First Century Books, 2001.

Pages: 64
Series: Great American Memorials

Ashabranner begins the book with a touching description of the dedication ceremony of the Korean War Veterans Memorial on June 25, 2000, and then describes the planning, funding, choice of site, and the controversy surrounding the memorial's design. A brief history of Korea and the war itself follows. A map of the country's topography and geography to clarify where Korea is located and what the terrain is like would have enhanced this section.

The process of creating the memorial is described, from the planning stage, funding, choice of site, design controversy, approval, construction, casting of the statues, to the completed memorial—a group of 19 stainless steel statues representing soldiers on patrol, a wall of remembrance, and a reflecting pool. The final chapter discusses how the memorial honors those who fought in the war, as well as its message to America.

The book ends with general information on the memorial's visiting hours and the bank of computers listing the dead, those missing in action, and those captured as prisoners during the war. The memorial Web site, address, and telephone number are provided. A Korean War chronology is included.

Glossary: No
Bibliography: Yes
Index: Yes
Level: Beginning New Readers

Ayer, Eleanor H. *The United States Holocaust Memorial Museum: America Keeps the Memory Alive.* New York: Dillon, 1994.

Pages: 79
Series: —

The reader is led on a floor-by-floor tour of the U.S. Holocaust Memorial Museum's unforgettable exhibits. Ayer, as tour guide, provides succinct information on the exhibits and on the events of the Holocaust. The pictures of the exhibits and the historical photographs convey the powerful effect the museum has on those who walk through it. The book includes a time line of the Holocaust.

Glossary: No
Bibliography: Yes, of secondary sources including books and
     periodicals
Index: Yes
Level: Beginning–Intermediate New Readers

Bailey, Gerry and Felicia Law. *Cowries, Coins, Credit: The History of Money.* Minneapolis, Compass Point Books, 2006.

Pages: 48
Series: —

Bailey and Law begin their exploration of the history of money with a two-page illustrated time line entitled "Landmarks in Money"— beginning with 9000–6000 BC, when cows were probably used as money, through to 1999, when the euro was adopted as Europe's single currency. Subsequent sections look at barter, first coins, coins from the 1200s to 1807, methods of record keeping and counting, the process of making money, coin collecting, the use of gold (including one-page explanations of the legend of El Dorado, Spanish gold, and pirates), mining and prospecting for gold, some gold mines of the world (a world map shows the locations of gold mines and lists the top mines in the world and the main gold-producing countries), treasure hunting, bullion, the gold standard, paper money, forgery, stamps, checks, plastic money, and international money and foreign exchange.

A generous number of highlighted boxes on such topics as the parts of a coin, alchemy, tobacco money, famous stamps, the Check 21 system of electronically scanning checks, credit card identity theft, and more supplement the text. Small fact boxes, plus a few lists and charts, are also included as are clear, detailed photos of coins, old notes, and stamps. The cartoon illustrations, accompanied by captions or short fact-filled notes, add a lighthearted touch for adult and younger readers. The book is a handy first source on the subject.

Glossary: Yes
Bibliography: Yes, of four children's books and Web sites
Index: Yes
Level: Beginning–Intermediate New Readers

Barnes, Trevor. *Kingfisher Book of Religions: Festivals, Ceremonies and Beliefs from Around the World.* New York: DIANE Publishing, 2001.

Pages: 160
Series: Kingfisher Book of . . .

A fascinating introduction to world religions, the author looks at the ancient religions of Egypt, Greece, and Rome as well as the traditional beliefs of Native Americans, Australian Aborigines, Maori, and and some African societies. There are chapters on such major religions as Hinduism, Buddism, Judaism, Christianity, and Islam and modern-day religious groups like the Mormons, Seventh-day Adventists, Jehovah's Witnesses, Baha'I, and Hare Krishna.

Each religion is described from its origins through its beliefs and rituals, festivals, ceremonies, places of worship, and where (in the world) it is practiced. A special look at the roles children play within each religion, to help illustrate the variety of different beliefs, is included. Rich with photographs and illustrations, charts, and cutaways, the book serves as a solid introduction to the subject.

Glossary: Yes
Bibliography: No
Index: Yes
Level: Intermediate New Readers

Brookfield, Karen. *Book*. Photographed by Laurence Pordes. (A Dorling Kindersley Book.) New York: Knopf, 2000.

Pages: 63
Series: Eyewitness Books

This title is an excellent example of how text and illustrations are blended together to provide a rich source of information on a multifaceted topic. The history of the origin of the book includes the development of writing, paper, printing, binding methods, the growth of literacy, the making of affordable books, the expansion of the book market, and the evolution of libraries. Each chapter appears on a richly illustrated two-page spread.

An introductory paragraph in large type is complemented by small-print explanations for each illustration. This exquisite tribute to books and writing gives readers a sense of viewing the actual artifacts arranged in a special museum exhibit.

Glossary: No
Bibliography: No
Index: Yes
Level: Beginning–Intermediate New Readers

DeCapua, Sarah. *The Vietnam Memorial*. New York: Children's Press, 2003.

Pages: 48
Series: Cornerstones of Freedom, Second Series

This poignant story of the birth of the idea for the Vietnam memorial and the unflagging efforts to make it a reality includes historical background on the war and its victims as well as information on the origins of the antiwar sentiment and those who suffered because of it. Veteran Jan C. Scruggs turned his vague idea for a memorial to all the American men and women who fought in Vietnam into reality after a difficult struggle for approval of his plan, congressional support, and the necessary funds. Maya Ying Lin, a young Yale University student who won the national design competition, visualized what the memorial should be like while visiting the site. The author briefly describes final approval of the design, the construction, the dedication, and the message the memorial gives to its many visitors—the sacrifices of those who fought in the war should always be remembered. The traveling replica produced in 1996, designed to bring "The Wall That Heals" to communities throughout the United States, is mentioned.

The color and black-and-white photographs enhance the text. An illustrated time line is included. This book is a good first source on the subject.

Glossary: Yes
Bibliography: Yes, of books, organizations, and Web sites
Index: Yes
Level: Beginning New Readers

Guzzetti, Paula. *The White House.* Parsippany, NJ: Dillon, 1996.

Pages: 72
Series: Places in American History

A map locating Washington, DC, a cutaway view of the White House, and photographs of the James Hoban design for the building, the East Room when it was used to hang wash during Abigail Adams's time, the gutted interior during the Truman administration, portraits of a few past and present residents, a number of the most well-known rooms, and the Rose Garden accompany a text rich with historical facts. The reader is taken on a memorable word-and-picture tour. The usefulness of the book is enhanced by a three-page chronology, beginning with 1789, the year Washington was elected, to 1993, when a jogging track was constructed on the grounds. A list of presidents and their dates in office and two pages of visitor information are included. This title is a quick reference source for adults.

Glossary: No
Bibliography: No
Index: Yes
Level: Beginning–Intermediate New Readers

Langley, Myrtle. *Religion.* New York: DK, 2005.

Pages: 72
Series: Eyewitness

The quest for the true nature of existence, the meaning of life and death, the origins of life, and the mystery of the universe are basic to the emergence of all religions. The author takes on the ambitious task of exploring the practices and sacred rituals of the world's major religions, as well as the role they play in different cultures—from the relationship between gods and nature in ancient Greece to the traditions and beliefs of Hinduism, Buddhism, Confucianism, Taoism, Shintoism, Jainism, Zoroastrianism, Judaism, Christianity, Islam, and more. Each section begins with a short introductory paragraph, followed by informative captions for the vivid color illustrations that fill the pages. There are quick reference boxes answering questions about the different religions—one God, the afterlife, founders, scriptures, and written code. A brief overview of the world's major religions, this book is a good quick reference source.

Glossary: No
Bibliography: No
Index: Yes
Level: Beginning–Advanced New Readers

LeVert, Suzanne. *The Electoral College.* New York: Franklin
Watts, 2004.

Pages: 64
Series: Watts Library

An exploration of why Al Gore, with the majority of popular votes, lost
the 2000 election to George W. Bush begins this explication of the
electoral college—citizens are not voting for their candidate of choice,
but for the state electors. The history of the presidential election
process, as framed in the Constitution, is traced from Washington's
election to the present. Disputes and changes that tested the electoral
college system are discussed, along with it's future: do away with it or
adopt one of a number of proposed changes. LeVert states that with
the next controversial election, this question will be debated yet again.
Fact boxes with additional information, numerous photo illustrations,
and a time line enrich the text. This is a solid, well-documented, and
concise look at the electoral college for readers confused by it.

Glossary: Yes, words included are in boldface throughout the text
Bibliography: Yes, of books, organizations, and Web sites, as well as
       an author's note on sources used to research the book
Index: Yes, numbers in italic indicate illustrations
Level: Beginning–Intermediary New Readers

Maestro, Betsy. *The Story of Religion.* Illustrated by Giulio
Maestro. New York: Clarion, 1996.

Pages: 48
Series: —

This book combines the story of religion with a lesson in religious
tolerance. It is an informative and absorbing introduction to the origin
of religious ideas and beliefs that led to early polytheistic practices (i.e.,
the spirit worship of early primitive peoples; the ancient Sumerian,
Egyptian, and Greek worship of multiple gods) and the great world
faiths: Chinese beliefs, Hinduism, Buddhism, Judaism, Christianity
(Roman Catholic, Eastern Orthodox, and Protestantism), and Islam.

The beliefs and practices of the various faiths are concisely explained in a well-illustrated text that flows along without chapter breaks. There are brief descriptions of the sacred books of Confucianism (the Analects), Hinduism (the Vedas), Buddhism (the Tripitaka or Pali Canon), Judaism (the Tanakh), Christianity (the Bible), and Islam (the Qur'an). Other sacred texts—including the Avesta of Zoroastrianism, the Kojiki of Shintoism, the Kitab Akdas of Baha'ism, the Tao Te Ching of Taoism, the Adi Granth of Sikhism, and the Siddhanta of Jainism—are listed. The festivals and holidays of the world religions, including Zoroastrianism, Jainism, Shintoism, and Sikhism, are described. The Golden Rule, as expressed by the world's major religions, is included to demonstrate that all of the faiths practice the same code of behavior. A good quick reference source, the book explains a complex subject in simple language.

Glossary: No
Bibliography: No
Index: Yes
Level: Beginning–Intermediary New Readers

Markovitz, Hal. *The Lincoln Memorial.* Philadelphia: Mason Crest, 2003.

Pages: 48
Series: American Symbols and Their Meanings

This clear, easy-to-read accounting of the lengthy struggle to erect a memorial to Abraham Lincoln takes the reader on a short tour of the monument, with emphasis on what it symbolizes. The author backs up to 1867 and the first plan for a memorial to Lincoln and then traces the history of its planning, development, construction, and completion. Facts about the people involved in authorizing federal money and the sculptor, artist, and architects are included—with biographical information in highlighted boxes. Fact boxes provide additional information.

The book opens and closes with a look at memorable events, Marian Anderson's performance in 1939 and the Martin Luther

King speech during the 1963 march on Washington. Color and black-and-white photographs complement the text. There is also a two-page chronology.

Glossary: Yes
Bibliography: Yes, of books and Internet resources
Index: Yes
Level: Beginning–Intermediate New Readers

Miller, Natalie. *The Statue of Liberty.* Danbury, CT: Children's, 1992.

Pages: 32
Series: Cornerstones of Freedom

This simple account of the Statue of Liberty progresses from the French sculptor Bartholdi's conception of the statue as a monument to the American belief in individual worth, freedom, and liberty to his trip to the United States for a government grant of land and his choice of Bedloe's Island as the site. The various design phases of the statue, the step-by-step creation of larger and larger plastic models, Alexandre Gustave Eiffel's design of a special skeleton to support the statue, and the building of the pedestal designed by Richard Morris Hunt, are detailed. The final assembly of Liberty and her dedication on October 28, 1886, are celebrated. Later problems preserving Lady Liberty, including the massive repair job begun in 1984 and the reopening in time for the statue's centennial celebration in 1986, are explored. This brief history is documented with photographs.

Glossary: No
Bibliography: No
Index: Yes
Level: Beginning New Readers

Moehn, Heather. *World Holidays: A Watts Guide for Children.* New York: Franklin Watts, 2000.

Pages: 123
Series: —

This book of more than 100 holidays, alphabetically arranged, provides brief facts about religious holidays, national observances, and festivals, such as those related to harvest and changing seasons. The author goes beyond the well-known religious holidays to discuss lesser-known Islamic, Hindu, Japanese, Jewish, and other observances. The secular holidays described include some unusual days, such as Baby's First Haircut (Bolivia), Berchtold's Day (Switzerland), King Kamehameha I Day (Hawaii), Mormon Pioneer Day (Utah and other states with a large Mormon population), Native American Indian Pow Wow (year-round in North America), and Waitangi Day (New Zealand).

Many entries include color illustrations with descriptive captions and cross-references to related entries in the book. A section on calendars from around the world includes clear descriptions of the Roman, Julian, Gregorian, Jewish, Hindu, Chinese, and Islamic calendars. A holiday calendar for the years 2001–2005 follows. If adults can disregard the subtitle identifying the book as a guide for children, they will find it a handy quick reference source.

Glossary: Yes
Bibliography: Yes
Index: Yes
Level: Beginning–Intermediate New Readers

Munro, Roxie. *The Inside–Outside Book of Libraries.* Paintings by Roxie Munro; text by Julie Cummins. New York: Dutton Children's Books, 1996.

Pages: 48
Series: Inside–Outside

Munro's wonderful paintings are blended with Cummins' text to demonstrate the richness and immeasurable value of all types of American libraries, from the simplest home library to the modern computerized library that offers access to a vast body of information via the Internet. The collections and services of the Chatham Square Library in New York City's Chinatown, the tiny Ocracoke Library in North Carolina, the Library of Congress, New York City's Andrew

Heiskell Library for the Blind and Physically Handicapped, the Explorers Club Library in New York City, the U.S. Navy's Abraham Lincoln (CVN72) Library located on an aircraft carrier, California's Folsom State Prison Library, the Berkeley California Public Library's Tool Lending Library, the Internet and the World Wide Web, the Meadows Elementary School Library in Plano, Texas, plus a variety of home libraries, bookmobiles, and the New York Public Library are introduced in descriptive text and accurate, detailed illustrations. An aesthetically appealing children's picture book of value to adults (particularly new readers and ESL students) as a brief guide to the treasures available in libraries of all sorts.

Glossary: No
Bibliography: No
Index: No
Level: Beginning New Readers

Orr, Tamra. *The Department of Transportation.* New York: Rosen, 2006.

Pages: 64
Series: This Is Your Government

A brief introduction defines the mission and function of the Department of Transportation (DOT), a cabinet-level government office headed by the secretary of transportation, who is appointed by the president and approved by Congress. A DOT organization chart is included in a brief introduction. Chapter 1 provides a concise history of the department, from its beginnings and the growth of transportation, its establishment on October 15, 1966, when President Johnson signed Public Law 89-670 (the Department of Transportation Act), through the Nixon, Carter, Reagan, Bush, Clinton, and G.W. Bush years. Chapter 2 looks at the achievements of a few of the 14 secretaries of transportation: Alan S. Boyd (1967–69), the first secretary to be appointed; Dr. Claude Stout Brinegar (1973–75), the third secretary, who dealt with the energy crisis; Brockman "Brock" Adams (1977–79), who had a major impact on automobile safety design and fuel economy standards; Elizabeth Hanford Dole (1983–87), who focused on safety-related issues, particularly air bag usage, safety belts, and rear window brake lights; and Norman Yoshio Mineta (2001–present), who helped draft the post 9/11 Aviation and Transportation Security Act. Chapter 3 concisely defines how the DOT works and explains the function of each of the 11 agencies within the department. Chapter 4 examines the role of the DOT in the twenty-first century.

A four-page time line, boxed pages with additional information, and captioned color photo illustrations supplement the text. This concise, fact-filled title provides a quick overview of a multifaceted agency.

Glossary: Yes
Bibliography: Yes, of books, government agencies, and Web sites
Index: Yes
Level: Beginning–Intermediate New Readers

Penney, Sue. *Christianity.* Chicago: Heineman, 2001.

Pages: 48
Series: World Beliefs & Cultures

This concise explication of Christianity progresses from a definition of Christian belief, with a brief discussion of Jesus, to a look at the early history and growth of Christianity, its division and reformation, denominations, and the fundamental differences between the Roman Catholic, Orthodox, and Protestant churches. A look at the Bible and its teachings, how Christians worship at home and in church, and some church buildings, pilgrimages, celebrations, and family occasions completes the text. Numerous fact boxes provide additional information (e.g., about St. Paul, Martin Luther, the Eucharist, and the World Council of Churches). The book is enhanced with many illustrations, a map of significant place names, and side-by-side time lines of major events in world and Christian history. This title is a useful source for a brief overview of a complicated subject.

Glossary: Yes, of words appearing in boldface throughout the text
Bibliography: Yes, of two titles
Index: Yes
Level: Beginning–Intermediate New Readers

Wilkinson, Philip. *Islam.* New York: DK, 2005.

Pages: 72
Series: Eyewitness

With characteristic brief introductions to each short chapter, abundant illustrations, and explanatory captions, the faith, culture, and history of Islam is examined from its beginnings in early Arabia to the emergence of the prophet Mohammad in 610, when the Qur'an was first revealed to him. The Qur'an (holy book of Islam), the five pillars of Islam, the mosque, caliphate, scholars and teachers, culture, the crusades, costume and jewelry, and, finally, festivals and ceremonies are discussed. Wilkinson has authored a memorable overview of a complex religion appropriate for adult readers.

Glossary: No
Bibliography: No
Index: Yes
Level: Intermediate New Readers

Wu, Dana Y. *Our Libraries.* Brookfield, CT: Millbrook, 2001.

Pages: 48
Series: I Know America

Where do you go to find information on any and every subject in books, online, or in any other medium? Public libraries provide access to the entire world of recorded knowledge, and the librarian provides the expertise to help locate any information sought—all of this, and more, for free.

The author explains the importance of libraries and touches on the collection (book and nonbook), the catalog, classification system, programs and services, access to computers, and special programs for immigrants, families, children, and handicapped. The author describes how libraries work and briefly summarizes the history of libraries in the United States. One chapter is devoted to the Library of Congress. In the final chapter, Wu discusses libraries in the information age—providing computers for Internet access, database searching, and word processing. The author emphasizes the need for increased funding and lists ways to support one's public library. The book includes photo illustrations with informative captions and highlighted pages that explain the Dewey Decimal System, Banned Books Week, and the Poet Laureate of the Library of Congress. A chronology is included.

Although the size of the book and large print indicate that this is a children's title, the pictures show people of all ages. This book is of interest for its brief, informative look at public libraries—it will not insult adult readers in need of a quick, easy-to-read reference to the subject.

Glossary: No
Bibliography: Yes
Index: Yes
Level: Beginning New Readers

❈ History and Geography ❈

Augustin, Byron and Jake Kubena. *Iraq.* New York: Scholastic, 2006.

Pages: 144
Series: Enchantment of the World, Second Series

This fact-filled title looks at Iraq's beginnings, its history (from ancient civilizations to modern times), geography, climate, environment, flora and fauna, and diverse population, and the Muslim nation. The authors discuss the Iraqi war and the present political situation and clearly define the differences between Shi'i Muslims, Sunni Muslims, and Kurds. The final chapter looks at the uncertain future of the country.

The book is rich with striking full-color illustrations, numerous maps, and highlighted illustrated fact boxes on related topics: dust storms, the date palm, Grand Ayatollah Ali Muhammad al-Sistani, and the fast of Ramadan. There is a time line of Iraqi history and world history running side by side on a two-page spread.

An illustrated "Fast Facts" section provides background data on the country: official name, capitol, official languages, official religion, year of founding, area, bordering countries, highest and lowest elevation and temperature, major rivers, population of largest cities, famous landmarks, industry, currency, literacy rate, common words and phrases, famous Iraqis, and more.

The text is enhanced with full-color photo illustrations, charts, and diagrams. This is a readable, updated reference source for researchers as well as adult general readers seeking to expand their knowledge of the country.

Glossary: No
Bibliography: Yes, of books, articles, Web sites, and the Iraqi
     embassy address and telephone number
Index: Yes
Level: Intermediate–Advanced New Readers

Aylesworth, Thomas G. and Virginia L. Aylesworth. *Southern New England: Connecticut, Massachusetts, Rhode Island.* New York: Chelsea House, 1995.

Pages: 64
Series: Discovering America

One volume of a series of books on the states and U.S. possessions and territories, this quick reference source provides answers to many frequently asked questions. For each state, a picture of the official seal is given, along with a one-sentence history of its origin. Other facts about each state include the flag, motto, capital, state name and nicknames, and the official flower, tree, bird, animal, insect, mineral, marine mammal, and song. The population, geography and climate, industry, agriculture, government, history, sports, major cities, places to visit, events to attend, famous people born in the state, and the locations and founding dates and enrollment figures of the state's colleges and universities are given, as well as where to obtain more information. A map of the state marking the capital, cities and towns, and places to visit is included, as is a smaller map of the United States showing the location of the particular state. The photographs provide clarification and additional information.

Glossary: No
Bibliography: Yes
Index: Yes
Level: Beginning New Readers

Bachrach, Susan D. *Tell Them We Remember: The Story of the Holocaust.* Boston: Little, Brown, 1994.

Pages: 128
Series: —

With poignant illustrations and transcribed oral and video histories from the United States Holocaust Museum, this book relates the horrors of the Holocaust. Special focus is placed on the young innocent victims who were murdered simply because they were considered inferior by Nazi Aryan master race standards. The text covers background history, the rise of Hitler, the ghettos, victim transports, the death camps, gas chambers, resistance movements and rescue, liberation, the Nuremberg trials, and the fates of survivors. A photo ID guide of young people follows the introduction. Their stories appear throughout the book in sidebars, with ID photos of individual children and teens repeated. The author reminds readers that others, such as gypsies, the disabled, the mentally ill, and homosexuals, were also victims of the death camps. This is a compelling photo history. The text and illustrations, and a chronology of events, capture the chilling events of this horrific period in history.

Glossary: Yes
Bibliography: Yes, of general overviews, specialized nonfiction
    topics, biographies, fiction, memoirs, and art, and a selection of
    titles, listed in the same categories, for more advanced readers
Index: Yes
Level: Intermediate–Advanced New Readers

Baquedano, Elizabeth and Barry Clark. *Aztec, Inca, and Maya.*
Illustrated by Michel Zabe. New York: DK, 2005.

Pages: 72
Series: Eyewitness Books

This is an excellent fact-filled introduction to the ancient Aztec and Mayan civilizations of Mesoamerica (central and southern Mexico, Yucatan, Guatemala, Belize, El Salvador, western Honduras, part of Nicaragua, and northern Costa Rica) and the Inca civilization of the west coast of South America (most of Peru, part of Ecuador and

Bolivia, northwest Argentina, and most of Chile). The two-page chapters are rich with maps, cutaway photographs, and clearly labeled captioned pictures that enhance the brief descriptive text. Among the subjects covered are farming, hunting and fishing, cities, family life, home life, food and drink, trade and tribute, the warrior, religious life, gods and goddesses, life after death, human sacrifice, medicine, writing and counting, weaving and spinning, clothes and accessories, pottery, feather work, precious metals and stones, masks, dance and music, sports and games, animal life, and the Spanish conquest. The next best thing to a museum tour, this book is an excellent source for facts about the Aztec, Inca, and Mayan peoples.

Glossary: No
Bibliography: No
Index: Yes
Level: Beginning–Intermediate New Readers

Bausum, Ann. *Our Country's Presidents.* Washington, DC: National Geographic, 2005.

Pages: 207
Series: —

Beginning with a solid introduction to American democracy and the institution of the presidency, this revised and expanded edition provides comprehensive profiles of the presidents from Washington to George W. Bush. It includes highlights of their administrations and their own achievements—presented in chronological order, grouped by historical periods, with an illustrated time line accompanying the essays. Introductory paragraphs list each president's major accomplishments. There are funny stories, unexpected facts, how presidents helped establish national traditions, memorable quotes from speeches, letters and diaries, and answers to the questions on who were the best and the worst leaders. Facts and events of each period, from wars to inventions, explorations to protests, are provided, and political terms are explained.

Quick reference fact boxes include data on political party; vice president; birth, inauguration, and death dates; first lady; nicknames; and more. Additional pages include events from the 2004 election, the war on terror, a history of the White House and a cutaway of the building, presidential powers, a chart of the three branches of government, a map of presidential landmarks, presidents who died in office, and a clear explanation of the electoral college. Marvelous photography and art, including official portraits of the presidents, political cartoons, artifacts, and pictures from each historical era, complement the text. This is a spectacular, authoritative resource for both general interest and research.

Glossary: No
Bibliography: Yes, and a resource guide
Index: Index: Yes, with boldface indicating illustrations
Level: Intermediate–Advanced New Readers

Blashfield, Jean F. *Washington.* New York: Children's Press, 2001.

Pages: 144
Series: America the Beautiful

The short introductory chapter has information on Washington's scenery, climate, business, life, a famous person (Jeff Bezos, founder of Amazon.com), a geographical map of Washington, and a fact box about the misnaming of the state. The history and exploration of the land and the growth of the state is described from the early years, through World War II, and on to the present—with mention of famous people, from presidents to Bill Gates. Other chapters include an overview of it's geographic features, natural resources, wildlife, climate, cities—focusing on Seattle—government, industry, people, and culture (sports and creative fun). Also provided is information on the state flag, seal, song, and symbols—including the state ship, the first to be adopted by any state. There is a "Fast Facts" section, numerous color and black-and-white photographs, highlighted fact boxes with supplementary information, and small easily read maps. Rich with information, this book provides readers with a solid view of the state of Washington.

Glossary: No
Bibliography: Yes, of books, Web sites, and state and government
    addresses
Index: Yes
Level: Beginning–Intermediate New Readers

Bockenhauer, Mark H. and Stephen F. Cunha. *Our Fifty States.* Foreword by Jimmy Carter. Washington, DC: National Geographic, 2004.

Pages: 239
Series: —

Packed with fascinating facts and figures, maps, illustrations, and essays about each state, this book is organized by region (Northeast, Southeast, Midwest, Southwest, and West) and then alphabetically by state within each region. The regional sections begin with a map identifying mountains, plains, rivers, and other geographic features that influence climate, natural resources, and population patterns. An essay on each region is followed by four-page sections devoted to each state within that region. These pages include a photo essay, an illustrated time line of significant events in the state's history, a full-page map, and a "state-at-a-glance" box that lists area, population, capital city, ethnic and racial makeup, major economic activities, nickname, statehood date and ranking by size and population, and some fun facts. Each state's motto, bird, and flower are included. There is a full-spread map of all 50 states, information on the District of Columbia and U.S. territories in the Carribean and the Pacific, and comparative charts. Quotes from famous writers capture the character of each region. Easy to use and comprehensive, this book is a joy to read.

Glossary: No
Bibliography: Yes, with more advanced books and Web sites

Index: Yes, detailed
Level: Intermediate–Advanced New Readers

Bolden, Tonya. *Cause: Reconstruction America, 1863–1877.* New York: Knopf, 2005.

Pages: 138
Series: —

The Civil War continues to be one of the most captivating periods in American history—indeed thousands of books have been published on the subject. Bolden points out that the post–Civil War era was a complex period of reconstruction and upheaval that deserves attention as well. This overview of the historical, political, and social climate that precipitated change examines Lincoln's Proclamation of Amnesty and Reconstruction; the Civil Rights Act of 1866; the question of whether any other than white men can be a part of American democracy; the troubles of freed slaves; the plight of Native Americans as the nation expanded west; the Fifteenth Amendment and women's rights; the status of immigrants, and more. The possibilities of this period of reconstruction were vast but the laws passed, while positive steps, fueled upheaval, violence, and oppression.

Cause is well written and rich with black-and-white photo illustrations that have detailed captions. There are also chapter notes. This impressive title serves as a general interest resource and research source.

Glossary: No
Bibliography: Yes
Index: Yes, page numbers in italic refer to illustrations
Level: Advanced New Readers

Bramwell, Martyn. *Europe.* Minneapolis, Lerner, 2000.

Pages: 48
Series: The World in Maps

This book begins with a map and a brief description of Europe, with a highlighted box defining the European Union. Brief sections covering each of the countries include a picture of its flag and fact boxes describing its status, area, population, capital, language, currency, and overseas territories. Basic information, touching on history, physical features, natural resources, economy, and energy resources, is provided for each country. Geographical and political maps and small captioned pictures, along with a land use map for Germany and Russia, a color-coded map of European Russia, one of temperatures for Russia, and a sidebar of events of the conflict in the former Yugoslavia through 1999, are included. The brief text is appealing. Despite the small size of the maps and the skimpy index, the format is handy for readers looking for basic information and maps of Europe brought together in one volume.

Glossary: Yes
Bibliography: No
Index: Yes
Level: Beginning New Readers

Clare, John D., ed. *The First World War.* San Diego: Harcourt Children's Books, 1995.

Pages: 64
Series: Living History

World War I mobilized over 65 million men from more countries than in any previous war, and it caused millions of deaths and terrible destruction. At the end of the war, the signers of the Treaty of Versailles placed the blame for the war on Germany, which paved the way for Hitler's rise to power and the start of World War II. Very readable, the book's history of the period provides a sense of the drama of the war. The text is augmented with pictures, a chart of the trench system, maps, and historic photographs. This title is an excellent source of information for adults.

Glossary: No
Bibliography: Yes, a two-page section discussing the many
    primary and secondary sources available and suggesting some

titles, films, and authors of fiction, poetry, and historical accounts
Index: Yes
Level: Intermediate New Readers

Cooper, Michael L. *Dust to Eat: Drought and Depression in the 1930s.* New York: Clarion, 2004.

Pages: 84
Series: —

Cooper takes readers through the 1930s period of economic depression and dust beginning with the 1929 stock market crash and on to the Dust Bowl disaster. The author chronicles the daily struggle for survival and the massive movement west. Migrants streamed into California's San Joaquin Valley in search of a place to live and work. Cooper includes information on John Steinbeck's investigation of migrant workers and his tour of the squatter camps. One of many photo illustrations shows a number of migrant tents put up behind a billboard advertising the film version of Steinbeck's *Grapes of Wrath.*

This abysmal period of American history began to fade with the end of World War II and Franklin Roosevelt's "New Deal for America"—followed by new laws, programs, and legislation. The book is rich with black-and-white photographs reproduced from the Library of Congress collection, many of which are by Dorothea Lange, who was famous for capturing the misery and despair of the period. Other illustrations include a map of the California migrant farming cycle, a San Joaquin Valley harvest synopsis, and newspaper headlines reflecting migrant problems. Source notes are listed by chapter. This well-written and researched book is an impressive history of the period as well as a guide to further research.

Glossary: No
Bibliography: Yes, of books, videos, and Internet resources and organizations

Index: Yes, boldface refers to illustrations
Level: Advanced New Readers

Fradin, Dennis Brindell. *The Founders: The 39 Stories Behind the U.S. Constitution.* Illustrated by Michael McCurdy. New York: Walker, 2005.

Pages: 162
Series: —

In the introduction, Fradin reveals that the United States was not spelled with a capital "U" and "S" in its first years because most Americans did not think the name was a proper noun or, in fact, a country at all. Significant information about the division among the states as they argued over the framing of the federal government—one that would be strong and balanced—follows. A brief look at each state, with basic information on its delegates (birth and death dates, age at signing, marriages, number of children, and age at death), is followed by a concise two- or three-page profile of each creator and signer of the constitution. McCurdy's scratchboard illustrations add to the colonial look of the book and help grab the reader's attention as the facts about the fascinating lives of the drafters and signers of the document are revealed state by state. Finally, the book ends with a photo reproduction of the first page of the Constitution, followed by the entire text of the document. This title serves as a solid overview as well as guide to further research.

Glossary: No
Bibliography: Yes
Index: Yes
Level: Intermediate–Advanced New Readers

Freedman, Russell. *In Defense of Liberty: The Story of America's Bill of Rights.* New York: Holiday House, 2003.

Pages: 196
Series: —

Freedman examines the first ten amendments of the Bill of Rights, referring back to English law and the Magna Carta. He demonstrates the flexibility of the document through discussions of landmark Supreme Court cases that infringed upon civil liberties such as abortion, racial and religious discrimination, freedom of speech, and capital punishment and on to present-day conflicts regarding Internet access, electronic spying capabilities and the question of national security, and individual freedom since 9/11. The author explains the origins of each amendment and provides examples of challenges to laws and historical judgments handed down by the Supreme Court.

There is a brief discussion of the evolution of the Constitution and Bill of Rights. The book is rich with actual examples of infringements upon Constitutional rights and quotes from Supreme Court cases. The pages are filled with black-and-white photo reproductions, many from the Library of Congress collection. Chapter notes and an index of Supreme Court cases are included. Beautifully designed, this is an excellent study that provides a clear understanding of a document that continues to protect civil liberties and individual freedom.

Glossary: No
Bibliography: Yes, of books and Web sites
Index: Yes
Level: Intermediate–Advanced New Readers

Grace, Catherine O'Neill. *The White House: An Illustrated History.* New York: Scholastic, 2003.

Pages: 144
Series: —

Grace addresses readers directly, as tour guide to visitors. With the White House Historical Association's cooperation, the author's tour provides a close-up view of the history and present operations of the White House in clear and concise language, along with informative illustrations and marvelous art and photography. The book begins with a foreword by Neil W. Horstman of the White House Historical Association, a brief introduction by Laura Bush, an explanation of the White House as a national symbol of freedom, and a look at the chief usher's function by the man who holds the position, Gary Walters. A magnificent double-page foldout picture introduces each of the book's five sections.

Chapter 1 presents the history and evolution of the structure. A cutaway gives the reader an inside view of important rooms seen on the tour, a look at the visitor's center, and a remarkable model of the edifice. Subsequent chapters provide a glimpse of what working, celebrating, and living at the White House is like. There is a room-by-room tour of the Library, Vermeil Room, China Room, Diplomatic Reception Room, the Entrance Hall and Cross Hall, the East Room, and the Green Room. In "Faces and Voices" pages, behind-the-scenes staff members describe their jobs—the president's photographer, press secretary to the first lady, the pastry chef, grounds superintendent, the director of the Marine Band, the director of the Visitor's Office, the tour officer, the chief floral designer, the horticulturalist and pet handler, and the Director of Presidential Student Correspondence. The epilogue, "The White House Album," lists all the presidents who occupied the White House from George Washington (he chose the site and selected the architect but never lived in it) to George W. Bush.

This volume is filled with fascinating facts and illustrations. It is a beautifully designed reference source that can also serve as a coffee table book.

Glossary: No
Bibliography: Yes, of books, Web sites, and videos
Index: Yes
Level: Intermediate–Advanced New Readers

Hakim, Joy. *All the People*. New York: Oxford University Press, 2003.

Pages: 208
Series: A History of US

Book ten of this series discusses the complexities of the post–World War II years at home and abroad and the people who influenced the direction of events as the country assumed its new role as primary world power while struggling to redefine the meaning of democracy, particularly with regard to civil rights. Every page of this book is chock-full of information, including cultural trends of the decades following the war such as fast food, drive-in movies, and entertainers like the Beatles, Bob Dylan, Aretha Franklin, and The Four Tops. Many illustrations, informative captions, margin notes, definitions of words, highlighted boxes with additional historical facts, and quotations further enrich the text. A chronology of events follows the text in this outstanding, completely absorbing book.

The nine previous books in the series are *The First Americans*; *Making Thirteen Colonies*; *From Colonies to Country*; *The New Nation*; *Liberty for All?*; *War, Terrible War*; *Reconstruction and Reform*; *An Age of Extremes*; and *War, Peace, and All That Jazz*.

Glossary: No
Bibliography: Yes
Index: Yes
Level: Intermediate–Advanced New Readers

Hakim, Joy. *War, Terrible War.* New York: Oxford University Press, 2006.

Pages: 260
Series: A History of US

Book six of this remarkable series is an irresistible, well-documented, and absorbing account of the events leading to the Civil War, the tragedy of the war itself, and the reality of its aftermath. The war experience is related through a collection of human-interest stories that explore why Americans fought Americans. Historical pictures, photographs, cartoons, posters, maps, boxed references, margin notes, definitions of terms, plus a section on the songs of the Civil War and a chronology of events add to the richness of this source. Because of the author's talent for recounting events in history that read like a novel, one cannot put down this book, and the other volumes in the series are highly appropriate for any adult.

Glossary: No
Bibliography: Yes
Index: Yes
Level: Intermediate–Advanced New Readers

Hicks, Donna E. *The Most Fascinating Places on Earth.* New York: Sterling, 2005.

Pages: 48
Series: —

This introduction to 51 natural and man-made wonders provides information on history, origins, statistical data (height, depth, length, scientific facts), the amazing people who created the phenomenon or discovered it, and a variety of interesting trivia. Each entry includes black-and-white drawings that clarify the text. Additional boxed data answer some fascinating questions, such as why Stonehenge was built, who was the first to reach the top of Mount Everest, what animals live in the Sahara, what the curved roofs of the Sydney Opera House are made of, how old the giant sequoia trees are, where the world's longest skating rink is located, and the number of steps inside the Statue of Liberty from the base to the torch. A world map at the front of the book locates the places discussed. Each section (North America, South America, Europe, Asia, Africa, Australia, Antarctica, and, collectively, the Galapagos Islands, Easter Island, and the Marianas Trench) begins with a similar location map. The book lists well-known wonders as well as some less common ones, such as Parliament Hill in Ottawa, Ontario, the Yukon Territory, Venice, and the Nile River.

A handy reference source on a popular subject, the book succeeds in whetting the appetite for further research. A list of other sources would have been helpful.

Glossary: No
Bibliography: No
Index: Yes
Level: Beginning–Intermediate New Readers

Krull, Kathleen. *V Is for Victory: America Remembers World War II.* Minneapolis: Sagebrush, 2002.

Pages: 115
Series: —

Written to commemorate the 50th anniversary of the World War II Allied victory, this fact-filled book comprehensively reviews this horrific time of mass murder, racial hatred, and world upheaval. The United States's effort to help win the conflict is discussed. The events leading up to the war in the European and Pacific theaters, the first days of American involvement, the fear that resulted in the disgrace of the Japanese-American internment camps, racial prejudice in the armed forces, and the Holocaust are among the topics touched upon. A section on the personalities of the war includes profiles of Franklin Delano Roosevelt, Eleanor Roosevelt, Adolf Hitler, Joseph Goebbels, Emperor Hirohito, General Hideki Tojo, Benito Mussolini, General Charles de Gaulle, General Dwight D. Eisenhower, General Douglas MacArthur, Ira Hayes (one of the marines photographed at the Iwo Jima flag raising), J. Robert Oppenheimer, and Harry S. Truman. A section on the weapons of the war, including pictures of the famous bombers built by various countries, is followed by a summary of the events that led to the war's end and to the emergence of the United States as the most powerful country in the world.

The book is richly illustrated with postcards, posters, newspaper headlines, personal letters, railway tickets, pictures of artifacts of the war, a war map of the nations, and photographs of many famous and infamous personalities, battle scenes, and victims of the war, including concentration camp inmates. An illustrated chronology follows the text. This book is a very readable, visually effective, extraordinary reference source.

Glossary: No
Bibliography: Yes, with books for young readers marked with an
     asterisk
Index: Yes
Level: Intermediate–Advanced New Readers

Lye, Keith. *The Complete Atlas of the World.* Austin, TX:
Raintree, 1995.

Pages: 160
Series: —

This easy-to-use atlas covers more than the usual maps of the countries of the world. It includes a view of the physical world, an up-to-
date map of the political world, and maps of the world's climatic
zones, habitats (showing the physical zones: ice and snow, tundra,
mountains/barren land, forest, grassland, semidesert, and desert),
environments under threat (showing locations of remaining tropical
rain forests, areas of tropical rain forest deforestation, deforested
areas at risk of desertification, and true desert), the world's population density and distribution, the world's energy resources and
mineral reserves, and the agricultural zones of the world. Clear
explanatory text accompanies each map and provides background
information. The two-page spreads for each of the different regions
of the world include facts about history, geography, politics, culture,
language, religion, styles of government, membership in international organizations, economic and welfare indicators (1990 figures),
area, population, currency, and flags. Instructions on how to use the
atlas are easy to follow.

Glossary: Yes
Bibliography: No
Index: Yes, as well as a gazetteer listing the places and features
     (such as mountains and rivers) located on the topographic map
     of each region
Level: Intermediate–Advanced New Reader

Parsons, Jayne, ed. *Geography of the World: The Essential Family Guide to Geography and Culture.* New York: DK, 2006.

Pages: 304
Series: —

This comprehensive book begins with a two-page illustrated guide to using the book, followed by brief discussions of the physical world, including moving continents, climate and vegetation, and the world population; and of the political world. The body of the book is divided into six sections based on the continents: North America, Central America and South America, Europe, Asia, Africa, and Australasia and Oceania. Each section has a map showing the entire continent and a "Things to Look for on the Map" highlighted box (including area, highest point, longest river system, largest island), and data on geographical features. A concise look at the peoples inhabiting each continent follows. Pages on individual countries are filled with facts on landscape, terrains, vegetation, history, climate, products, industry, agriculture, and more. There is a highlighted box for each country listing its capital city, area, population, official language(s), major religions, government, currency, adult literacy rate, life expectancy, people per doctor, and number of televisions per thousand people but fails to provide income and infant mortality figures.

A reference section looks at political systems (noting that no two countries have identical ones); natural disasters that shaped both human history and the landscape (including a list of major international aid organizations); the two major groups that divide the world's major faiths, the Western tradition and the Eastern tradition; health; education; rich and poor countries; and world trade.

This title is well organized and beautifully illustrated with detailed maps, a gazetteer, captioned full-color photographs and art on each page, fact lists, and "Find Out More" boxes at the end of each country listing other pages in the book that have more information on a particular subject. Recently revised and updated, the book is an informative, easy-to-use reference source for all ages.

Glossary: Yes
Bibliography: No
Index: Yes
Level: Beginning–Advanced New Readers

Pelta, Kathy. *California.* Minneapolis: Lerner, 2004.

Pages: 84
Series: Hello U.S.A.

Readers are taken on a quick tour of the state to learn about climate, terrain, flora and fauna, and its four geographical regions. The book summarizes California's history, culture, economy, and environmental problems and lists some famous Californians and facts about the state—nickname, state flower, tree, bird, animal, song, population, area, capital, major cities, number of congressional representatives and senators, some famous places to visit, natural resources, agricultural products, manufactured goods, wildlife, demographic data on where Californians work, as well as a California recipe.

A double-page section provides a few unusual facts about the state. For example, San Francisco's Golden Gate Bridge, spanning 6,450 feet, is one of the longest suspension bridges in the world; Levi's denim jeans were first made in California in 1874; and artificial "safequakes" at Universal Studios in Los Angeles and at the San Francisco planetarium allow visitors to learn what an earthquake feels like. The author includes a historical time line and a list of annual events, and almost every page contains photographs and maps—political and physical maps, one of Native American nations in the state, and an economic map.

Glossary: Yes
Bibliography: Yes, of books and Web sites
Index: Yes
Level: Intermediate–Advanced New Readers

Romano, Amy. *A Historical Atlas of the United States and Its Territories.* New York: Rosen, 2005.

Pages: 64
Series: The United States Historical Atlases of the Growth of a New
  Nation

This impressive atlas begins with an introduction to the history of U.S. growth as a result of exploration and expansion. At the same time, other territories were acquired as a result of war or as protection against the threat of war. There are three unincorporated territories (Guam, American Samoa, the U.S. Virgin Islands), two independent commonwealths (Puerto Rico and the Northern Mariana Islands), and dozens of uninhabited, or sparsely inhabited, islands around the world—adding about 4,000 square miles of land to the country's total area.

Chapter 1 explains the terms *incorporated territories, unincorporated territories*, and *commonwealth*; names the islands and atolls that fall into each category; and identifies modern acquisitions. Chapter 2 discusses Guam, and subsequent chapters cover Puerto Rico, American Samoa, the U.S. Virgin Islands, the Northern Mariana Islands, and lesser known territories such as Wake Island, Midway Island, Baker Island, Howland Island, Jarvis Island, Johnston Atoll, Kingman Reef, Palmyra Atoll, and Navassa Island. Information on early inhabitants, location, culture, economy and political control, and modern growth is provided. The full-color historical maps, photo illustrations (with informative captions), and highlighted illustrated fact boxes on Magellan, the Chamorro, the Spanish-American War, Puerto Rico, pirates, privateers, and buccaneers of the Carribean Islands enhance the text. A time line is included. This is an excellent source for information in one well-formatted volume.

Glossary: Yes
Bibliography: Yes, Web sites and three books for further reading
Index: Yes
Level: Beginning–Intermediate New Readers

Rubel, David. *Scholastic Encyclopedia of the Presidents and Their Times.* New York: Scholastic Reference, 2005.

Pages: 256
Series: —

Easy to use and read, this updated (to include results of the 2004 election) encyclopedia provides a wealth of information on the presidents along with an excellent history of the United States. Arranged by year, with one page for each year there was a president, the outside column of each page describes the political history of the presidency (laws passed, wars fought, treaties signed, and more), while the inside column looks at developments in the arts, medicine, science, industry, culture, and society. The presidents' early years, the first ladies, and milestones in the arts, science, medicine, industry, culture, and society are outlined. Brief facts about each president— birth and death dates, birthplace, party affiliation, vice president(s), wives, children, and nickname—appear in a box at the top of the page. Each president's full name and the years he was in office are also provided.

Additional features include photographs of the presidents; maps showing the growth of the United States with the year each state entered the Union; a table of presidential election results with term dates, names of vice presidents, the election candidates and party affiliations, the popular vote totals (beginning in 1824), and the total number of electoral votes; and an illustrated history of the White House. This absorbing reference source invites browsing.

Glossary: No
Bibliography: No
Index: Yes, with page numbers indicating where the most detailed
    explanations of particular subjects can be found
Level: Intermediate–Advanced New Readers

Scott, Elaine. *Poles Apart: Why Penguins and Polar Bears Will Never Be Neighbors.* New York: Viking, 2004.

Pages: 64
Series: —

This modest, attractive book explores the differences between the Arctic region and Antarctica in a completely engaging fashion. The introduction cites Captain Robert Falcon Scott's (British Royal Navy) diary entries of 1912 as he and his party made their way to the South Pole, marching in brutally frigid weather. He was filled with hope of reaching his destination, but the last entry indicates that he was aware that they all might perish—as they did. Today, the author points out, explorers have been replaced by scientists looking for answers to questions about the earth's magnetic field, the drift of the continents, climate changes, and more.

Nine chapters discuss the "poles apart" places—Antarctica, the earth's coldest continent; and the Arctic region, located in the frigid sea. Geographic locations and seasons, magnetism, the people (Inuit) of the North and the unpopulated South Pole, the explorers who preceded today's scientists, and the Antarctic Polar Station are examined. Of course, there is a chapter on penguins and one on polar bears. Together they explain why the two will never be neighbors. The book is rich with beautiful full-color and archival black-and-white photographs and reproductions as well as maps. All are captioned, adding more information for the reader. This impressive geographic history of the two regions is well written and memorable.

Glossary: No
Bibliography: Yes, books and Web sites
Index: Yes
Level: Intermediate–Advanced New Readers

Smith, Carter, ed. *The Revolutionary War: A Sourcebook on Colonial America.* Minneapolis: Lerner, 1991.

Pages: 96
Series: American Albums from the Collections of the Library of
   Congress

The historical, political, social, and cultural aspects of the Revolutionary War are examined through reproductions of original sources—documents, maps, prints, drawings, engravings, and broadsides from the Library of Congress collection. The brief introduction includes a map of the colonies, the dates of the war and of the northern and southern campaigns, names and dates of important battles, the total number of American and British soldiers killed or wounded, and the cost of the war to the British (about $500 million) and to the Americans (about $200 million).

The text is divided into three parts: Part I, April 1775 through June 1776, discusses the beginning of the fight for a new nation; Part II, July 1776 through January 1778, traces the American struggle for survival against the British after the Declaration of Independence is written; and Part III, February 1778 through February 1783, highlights the events that lead to victory. Each section has an illustrated time line of major events in world and colonial history. Among the documents reproduced are the front cover of Thomas Paine's *Common Sense*; George Washington's commission from the Continental Congress, naming him as "Commander in Chief of the United Colonies"; Jefferson's first draft and the completed Declaration of Independence; the first page of the Articles of Confederation; and "The Articles of Capitulation," the document of surrender signed by Cornwallis and Washington. The result is a totally absorbing, scholarly, visual history.

Glossary: No
Bibliography: Yes, of suggested readings and picture locations
    within the Library of Congress collections
Index: Yes, with page references to illustrations in italics
Level: Intermediate–Advanced New Readers

Stewart, Mark. *Uniquely New York.* Chicago: Heinemann, 2003.

Pages: 48
Series: Heinemann State Studies

The first chapter sums up the uniqueness of New York in brief text, photos of the Statue of Liberty and Niagara Falls, a small "Things to See" map of the state and New York City's five boroughs, and a highlighted box listing some unique facts about the state. Subsequent chapters briefly describe the state's symbols (seal, flag, bird, mammal, fish, and more), government, food and restaurants, culture, legends and lore (i.e., Rip Van Winkle, haunted houses, UFOs), sports (with a handy list of baseball, football, hockey, and basketball teams that are here today or long gone and those that moved out of state), business and products, attractions and landmarks, and notable buildings and structures. Ample small photographs dot the pages, along with small maps. New York's government organization is charted, and a number of fact boxes provide additional information on the state quarter, New York City's pushcarts, the "alligators in the sewers" legend, the Amityville Horror, New York City businesses, Jonas Salk and the polio vaccine, colleges and universities, and the Statue of Liberty. Attractive, this small book serves as a handy quick reference source.

Glossary: Yes
Bibliography: Yes
Index: Yes
Level: Beginning–Intermediate New Readers

Sutcliffe, Andrea. *The New York Public Library Amazing World Geography: A Book of Answers for Kids.* Hoboken, NJ: John Wiley, 2002.

Pages: 172
Series: The New York Public Library Answer Books for Kids

Answers to world geography questions are listed in sections, beginning with the world as a whole and followed by North and Central America, South America, Europe, Asia, Africa, Oceania, and Antarctica. The questions go beyond the expected highest–lowest, hottest–coldest, tallest–smallest records to include explorers, discoveries, origins of names, political boundaries, definitions of terms (i.e., apartheid, monsoon, chunnel), cultures, languages, landscapes, natural resources, and more. Black-and-white maps, charts and photos, fact boxes, and marginal notes complement the text. A list of world countries and territories provides data on areas, the capitals, governments, populations, and languages. Adults should ignore the "For Kids" in the subtitle, because they will enjoy browsing or, with the index, using the book as a quick reference source.

Glossary: Yes
Bibliography: Yes, as well as a recommended reading list and
     Internet resources
Index: Yes, with page numbers in italics indicating maps or
     illustrations
Level: Beginning–Intermediate New Readers

Viola, Herman J. *It Is a Good Day to Die: Indian Eyewitnesses Tell the Story of the Battle of the Little Big Horn.* New York: Crown, 2001.

Pages: 101
Series: —

A former director of the National Anthropological Archives, Viola presents exerpts from eyewitness accounts of Native Americans (leaders such as Sitting Bull and Antelope Woman and other participants) who took part in the battle identified by Native Americans as the "Battle of Greasy Grass" and by whites as "Custer's Last Stand." The 1876 battle at the Little Big Horn River, although a resounding victory for the Great Plains Indians, was ultimately a loss for them—they were pursued by cavalry until forced to surrender, with most going to live on reservations.

     The accounts are sandwiched between an introduction and an epilogue that provide an overview of events leading up to and following the battle itself. It is a bit difficult to picture the logistics of the battle, even with the aid of the maps included in the introduction. The book does, however, provide a glimpse of some aspects of Native American culture, customs, and psychology. Only the introduction and epilogue have a few small black-and-white photo reproductions. Biographical notes identify the various eyewitness speakers. A chronology is followed by a note on sources. This is a memorable first-hand account of a chaotic and violent event that contributed to the destruction of Native American life and culture.

Glossary: No
Bibliography: Yes
Index: Yes
Level: Advanced New Readers

Wilkinson, Philip and Michael Pollard. *The Magical East.*
Illustrated by Robert R. Ingpen. New York: Chelsea House, 1994.

Pages: 96
Series: Mysterious Places

This book gives a grand tour of some of the most fascinating ancient places of the East: Mohenjo-Daro, India (c. 2400–1800 BC); the Great Wall, China (c. 300 BC–AD 50); Yoshinogari, Japan (c. 300 BC–AD 300); Ellora, India (c. 600–900); Nara, Japan (c. 710–795); Angkor, Kampuchea (c. 900–1150); Easter Island, Oceania (c. 1100–1680); Great Zimbabwe, Zimbabwe (c. 1200–1450); the Forbidden City, Beijing, China (c. 1404–1450); and the Taj Mahal, Agra, India (c. 1632–1643). A descriptive text discusses the places (their phenomenal buildings and the lost or changed civilizations that created them) and the peoples and their cultures, religious beliefs, art, rulers, battles, societies, and more.

Much supplementary information in boxes enriches the contents, for example the origin of much of the wealth of Mohenjo-Daro; the enemies against whom the Great Wall of China was built; and the earthquake-resistant quality of the Japanese pagoda. The first page of each section has a "Did You Know?" box that highlights an interesting fact, a locator map, and a time line; and maps and color illustrations elucidate the text. A list of museums that display artifacts is included.

Glossary: No
Bibliography: Yes
Index: Yes
Level: Intermediate New Readers

Wills, Charles. *A Historical Album of Connecticut.* Minneapolis: Lerner, 1995.

Pages: 64
Series: Historical Albums

A brief introduction summarizes the significance of Connecticut in U.S. history. A small state (a little over 5,000 square miles), Connecticut was founded by Puritans moving southwest from Massachusetts. The state led the movement toward independence; played an important role in the Revolutionary War and the formation of the Union; was a leader in the country's industrial revolution because of the inventions of such citizens as Eli Whitney, Samuel Colt, and Seth Thomas; and grew to become a major twentieth century industrial region.

The first part of the book traces the history of the state from its early days as a colony through to the nineteenth century, when Hartford became the insurance capital of the nation. The second part focuses on the political, economic, and social problems that influenced growth and change from the nineteenth century to the present and includes a current profile of the state of the state. The book is well illustrated with photographs, prints, and engravings. Basic facts about the state (land area, climate, population, ethnic profile, flag, seal, motto, bird, etc.) are provided in a gazetteer following the text. Key events in the state's history and in American history, and very brief biographies of famous personalities, are included. An excellent quick reference source, this and other volumes in this series provide a nicely packaged mix of historic and contemporary state profiles.

Glossary: No

Bibliography: Yes, along with the names, addresses, and telephone
  numbers of two sources for further information

Index: Yes, with page numbers in italics indicating illustrations

Level: Beginning New Readers

Language Arts and Communications

Burns, Peggy. *The News.* Chicago: Raintree/Heinemann, 1995.

Pages: 32
Series: Stepping Through History

Large print, clear photographs, and concise, readable text are combined to provide a wealth of information about the history of journalism. Methods of passing on news are chronicled from the ancient cave paintings and scratched tablets of thousands of years ago to the invention of printing, the telegraph, newspapers, television, telefacsimile (fax), computer storage and transmission, fiber-optics, and satellite transmission of both print and graphics. A single-page chronology gives an overview of the development of methods of spreading the news. The address of the Museum of Broadcasting and other sources of information complete this marvelous book. Although now somewhat dated, this title remains an informative source for both reference use and pleasure reading about the development of communication.

Glossary: Yes, defining words in boldface and italic found within the text
Bibliography: Yes
Index: Yes, to both text and illustrations
Level: Beginning New Readers

Cooper, Kay. *Why Do You Speak as You Do? A Guide to Learning About Language.* New York: Walker, 1992.

Pages: 66
Series: —

The author begins her compact discussion of the phenomenon of language by defining what it is—the use of sounds to communicate thoughts, ideas, and feelings to others. She goes on to discuss what it is like to hear the sounds of strange languages and how these unique, often difficult-to-pronounce sounds become language. Theories of the development of language and how language changed as people began to migrate to different parts of the world are summarized. Word similarities among various languages are pointed out, for example, the English *mother,* the Latin *mater,* the Spanish *madre,* the German *mutter,* and the Russian *mat.* A concise definition of the origins and variations of English, from Old English to the regional accents of the United States, is followed by a discussion of how one learns to speak a language and an overview of the languages from which many English words are derived. Summaries of such languages as Chinese, Japanese, Vietnamese, Korean, Hebrew, German, French, and those of the American Indians are provided, as is a definition of an official language.

A readable introduction to linguistics is made even more engaging by cartoon illustrations. A good source for new adult readers, this book will be particularly helpful to those learning English as a second language.

Glossary: Yes
Bibliography: No
Index: Yes
Level: Beginning–Intermediary New Readers

Foresman, Scott. *Roget's Student Thesaurus,* rev. ed.
San Francisco: Pearson Scott Foresman, 1997.

Pages: 536
Series: —

This book begins with a two-page guide to understanding a thesaurus entry, information about choosing synonyms and why there are so many of them, and a list of the many excellent features that follow. "Around the World" provides words, phrases, and proverbs from a variety of cultures and languages; "Have You Heard . . . ?" gives the full meaning of familiar phrases and sayings; "Idioms" lists idiomatic expressions; "Verbs Plus" provides special phrases that combine a verb with another word; "Words At Play" shows how words can be humorous and entertaining; "Writer's Choice" explains the effectiveness of words, giving examples by well-known writers; "Watch It!" singles out words that may have derogatory meanings; "Word Story" explains the origins of English words; "Word Pool" provides words that share a similar meaning but are not synonyms; "Notable Quotable" quotes writers who use synonyms in interesting ways; "Writing Tip" gives hints on ways to improve writing; and "Word Workshop" uses different synonyms to improve writing. The book ends with an essay on creative writing and a writer's guide.

In the main text, entry words appear in boldface. Their parts of speech are identified, and synonyms with their definitions and example sentences, cross-references, antonyms, and slang words with the same meaning are included. The lighthearted illustrations support the aim of making this reference tool pleasant to use. The word "student" in the title can easily encompass adults beginning English and beginning writing students.

Glossary: No
Bibliography: No
Index: Yes, of synonyms, idioms, phrasal verbs, and features
Level: Advanced New Readers

Lang, Paul. *The English Language Debate: One Nation, One Language?* Berkeley Heights, NJ: Enslow, 1995.

Pages: 112
Series: Multicultural Issues

This is a well-documented exploration of the multifaceted question of whether or not English should be the only language of this nation of immigrants. The history of this controversial issue is traced from colonial times, when it became clear to the Germans (the second largest group of colonists) and other immigrants that a knowledge of English was essential to the enjoyment of all the economic, social, cultural, and political advantages the country had to offer. The one-language movement is rooted in the nation's motto, which has been stamped on every coin for 120 years: "E Pluribus Unum," meaning "Out of Many, One." That is, one nation, one goal, one philosophy, and, by extension, one language are essential to living, working, and learning together in harmony. In the 1790s, Congress took a step in this direction by voting that all laws were to be printed only in English. From these early times to the present, the one-language idea became intertwined with bigotry: Native Americans were savages; African slaves were not to be taught English; German and French immigrants were suspicious peoples; Mexicans were "know nothings"; and Hispanics, Chinese, Irish, and other groups of immigrants helping to develop this country were thought to be inferior and unwilling to assimilate into American society. Lang presents all sides of the argument by referring to case studies, providing examples of the viewpoints both for one language and for bilingualism, and examining the political impact on the controversy and educational theories on methods of teaching English. Land also touches on the negative economic impact resulting from Americans' lack of knowledge of a foreign language. This is a sobering, thought-provoking, well-documented text complete with chapter notes and a list of organizations that support official English and limitations on immigration and of those championing the opposite viewpoint of immigrant and language minority rights.

Glossary: Yes
Bibliography: Yes, of books, magazine and newspaper articles
Index: Yes
Level: Intermediate–Advanced New Readers

O'Reilly, Gillian. *Slangalicious: Where We Got That Crazy Lingo.*
Illustrated by Krista Johnston. New York: Annick, 2004.

Pages: 88
Series: —

Despite the book's framework as an unnamed protagonist's school assignment of exploring slang terms on the Internet—with help from Lexie and Edmond, two slang experts residing in the Internet—this book will intrigue adults too. It clearly defines the origins of 500 slang words and expressions, in a variety of categories (such as food, sports, and entertainment), in a way that brings language to life. Many slang words and expressions have long histories; some were low class, coarse words that achieved legitimate status, and others had various meanings as usage evolved. If the adult reader can put the playful, and perhaps too cute, presentation in the background, the value of the book will emerge. It contains an abundance of fascinating information. Numerous fact boxes provide additional related information, such as English slang words from other languages; definitions and origins of common terms, such as the beat generation, buck, salt money, corny, and musical and rhyming slang; and "Krieg and Blitz," slang with wartime/military origins.

Glossary: No
Bibliography: Yes, including adult titles and Web sites
Index: Yes
Level: Intermediate New Readers

Scholastic, Inc. *Scholastic Dictionary of Synonyms, Antonyms, and Homonyms.* New York: Scholastic, 2001.

Pages: 220
Series: —

A handy reference source of modest size, this book contains 12,000 synonyms, 10,000 antonyms, and 2,000 homonyms. The main entries, with the words being defined highlighted in boldface, list synonyms first, followed by antonyms in parentheses and italics. The second section lists potential problem words and their homonyms to clear up spelling confusion, for example, martial, in warfare, versus marshall, the officer; and yew, the tree, versus you, the person, versus ewe, the sheep. This is a ready-reference source when full dictionary definitions are not required.

Glossary: No
Bibliography: No
Index: No
Level: Intermediate–Advanced New Readers

Terban, Marvin. *Checking Your Grammar.* New York: Scholastic, 1993.

Pages: 144
Series: —

A guide to English, a tricky language with all sorts of grammatical rules and exceptions daunting to both young readers and adults, this reference source explains types of sentences, effective ways of building sentences, and subject–verb agreement. Parts of speech are succinctly defined. Many examples, the use of boldface for emphasis, some cartoon illustrations, the excellent page format, and "see also" notes in the margin to other sections of the book are effectively combined to impart information. All contribute to a realization that checking the rules of grammar need not be an unpleasant chore.

The section on style and usage serves as a guide to the rules of punctuation, capitalization, and spelling. There are also chapters on preventing double negatives, avoiding sexist language, and properly using homonyms, easily confused and misused words, contractions, compound words, idioms, acronyms, and abbrieviations. A list of common grammatical errors and their solutions is quite useful. This title is an easy-to-use guide for adults new to reading and writing English.

Glossary: No
Bibliography: No
Index: Yes
Level: Beginning New Readers

Terban, Marvin. *It Figures: Fun Figures of Speech.* Minneapolis: Sagebrush, 1993.

Pages: 61
Series: —

This book is a lighthearted lesson on how to effectively use the six figures of speech—simile, metaphor, onomatopoeia, alliteration, hyperbole, and personification—to add dimension and zing to thoughts, feelings, actions, characters, scenes, and events. Each figure of speech is clearly defined and explained with examples from the writings of some well-known authors, such as Ben Franklin, Clement Moore, Alfred Noyes, William Thackeray, and Shakespeare, along with Terban's own humorous creations. He builds on "Clowning Around," an absurd story about Clara, the crazy clown, by adding examples of the use of each figure of speech to embellish it. The cartoons, practice exercises, and the author's own suggestions further clarify the text. Terban presents a lively, totally painless discussion of the six figures of speech that adults frequently do not understand.

Glossary: No
Bibliography: Yes
Index: No
Level: Intermediate New Readers

Terban, Marvin. *Mad as a Wet Hen! And Other Funny Idioms.* Minneapolis: Sagebrush, 1987.

Pages: 64
Series: —

The obscure meanings of idioms cause much confusion for literal-minded people as well as those learning English for the first time. The most common idioms (130 of them printed in boldface) are effectively defined in one or two very short sentences and humorous illustrations. Unproven, as well as some rather unbelievable origins, of selected idioms follow. They are entertaining and serve to clarify meaning. For example, the expression "Let's talk turkey" supposedly derives from a day when a Pilgrim and an American Indian went hunting together. At the end of the day they wanted to divide the birds they caught so they had to "talk turkey." The book is divided into subject sections, including animals, body parts, feelings, colors, food, and hats. There is a useful alphabetical list of the idioms. This title is an enjoyable reference source for adults and student readers.

Glossary: No
Bibliography: Yes, of adult and juvenile sources
Index: No, but an alphabetical list of the idioms in the book lists page numbers
Level: Intermediate New Readers

Terban, Marvin. *Scholastic Dictionary of Idioms*. New York: Scholastic, 1998.

Pages: 256
Series: —

This list of idioms, more extensive than in the author's *Mad as a Wet Hen*, explains the meanings and the most accepted origins of over 600 expressions. Arranged in alphabetical order, the idioms appear in large boldface type. Each one is used in a sentence, with the idiom highlighted in yellow. A brief, clearly stated meaning is followed by a short paragraph on the origin of the expression. Some derive from fables, the ancient Greeks and Romans, authors such as Chaucer and Shakespeare, Native American customs, African-American speech, colloquialisms, or proverbs. The cartoon figures of children that appear on each page do not detract from the book's value as a quick reference source for adults.

Glossary: No
Bibliography: No
Index: Yes, alphabetical, with a separate key word index
Level: Advanced New Readers

Young, Sue. *Scholastic Rhyming Dictionary.* New York: Scholastic, 1994.

Pages: 213
Series: —

An easy-to-use format and modest size make this rhyming dictionary an attractive reference tool for adults with an interest in poetry. Words are listed by the beginning vowel of the rhyming sound, which is printed in large, boldfaced blue letters. The section on how to use the book explains that a rhyme can be located by looking directly under the particular sound or by looking the word up in the index to find under what sound it is listed. A concise explanation of rhyme enhances the book. Running headings, lighthearted cartoon illustrations, and white, gray, and light blue colors that highlight the various entries on each page simplify the reader's search for appropriate entries.

Glossary: No
Bibliography: No
Index: Yes, an alphabetical list of words and their related rhyming
    sounds
Level: Advanced New Readers

❊ Medicine and Health ❊

Cefrey, Holly. *AIDS.* New York: Rosen, 2001.

Pages: 64
Series: Epidemics

Cefrey presents an overview of AIDS (acquired immunodeficiency syndrome) that touches on all aspects of the disease. She begins with a history of AIDS and HIV (human immunodeficiency virus) and then discuss myths about the disease, causes and symptoms, diagnosis (including the stages of HIV and AIDS), how it is spread and not spread, the growth of the worldwide epidemic, treatment, research, and prevention.

    A number of captioned photo illustrations (including how AIDS attacks the immune system), a time line, and a profile of the two researchers named as codiscoverers of AIDS, add to the book's usefulness. Informative, but not preachy, the book serves as a basic guide and starting point for further research of the topic.

Glossary: Yes
Bibliography: Yes, of books and organizations in the United States
    and Canada
Index: Yes
Level: Intermediate New Readers

Davidson, Sue and Ben Morgan. *Human Body Revealed.*
New York: DK, 2002.

Pages: 38
Series: Revealed

This marvelously illustrated title is rich with unique medical images and graphics created with computer imaging techniques. Peel-away transparent pages are beautifully captioned and create a multi-dimensional look. The reader is taken on a tour of the human body to explore its inner workings—cells, chromosomes and DNA, the head, brain, eyes, ears, nose, mouth, the chest, lungs, heart, bloodstream, ribs, spine, the abdomen, liver, stomach, colon, esophagus, body chemistry, digestion, the pelvis, legs, bones, and skin. Two-page spreads focus on the different body systems, their anatomy and functions. Each section features a brief introductory paragraph, concise definitions, and explanations. This book provides an impressive close-up view of human physiology. It serves as an excellent reference source on a high-interest topic.

Glossary: No
Bibliography: No
Index: Yes
Level: Beginning New Readers

Demetriades, Helen A. *Bipolar Disorder, Depression, and Other Mood Disorders.* Berkeley Heights, NJ: Enslow, 2002.

Pages: 112
Series: Diseases and People

The book begins with a short profile of mood disorders—what they are, who gets them, and their causes, symptoms, prevention, and treatment. The author then discusses in more detail the causes, symptoms, and treatment of bipolar disorder and depression in terms of their physiological, genetic, and environmental relationships. Manic episodes are differentiated from depressive episodes. Various approaches to treatment are identified—insight therapies, behavior therapies, and biomedical, drug, and electroconvulsive therapies. The history of mood disorders is traced, along with stereotypes and myths, and future research is described.

Black-and-white illustrations, charts, case studies, and a few diagrams enhance the text. An information box lists steps to reducing stress.

A question and answer section, mood disorder time line, and chapter notes are included. This is a concise, well-researched overview useful as a quick guide to the subject as well as a starting point for further reading.

Glossary: Yes
Bibliography: Yes, of books and a separate list of organizations
Index: Yes
Level: Intermediate New Readers

Farndon, John. *1000 Facts on Human Body.* Steve Parker, Consultant. New York: Barnes & Noble, 2002.

Pages: 224
Series: 1000 Facts

This is a handy collection of brief explanations and definitions of numerous aspects of the human body, such as genes, thinking and the brain, the anatomy of the eye, the liver, diet, antibodies, transplants, and exercise. The book is rich with captioned illustrations and fascinating fact boxes that clarify some descriptions. Also included are facts about new medical technology. This title is ideal for adults looking for brief information, as well as for browsing.

Glossary: No
Bibliography: No
Index: Yes
Level: Beginning–Advanced New Readers

Gates, Phil. *History News: Medicine.* Milwaukee, WI: Gareth Stevens, 2001.

Pages: 32
Series: —

Written as a special edition newspaper, this book provides factual information on medical breakthroughs in the battle against disease, from trepanning as done in 8000 BC through Chinese acupuncture;

Roman ideas of hygiene; Indian nose surgery in 600 BC; the plague of the Middle Ages; the emergence of anatomy as a research subject; the discoveries of anesthesia, germs, X-rays, and penicillin; to the present times and organ transplantation, magnetic resonance imaging, gene therapy, and more. Some major figures, such as Galen, Pasteur, Jenner, and Nightingale, and lesser known doctors like Susruta (Indian doctor who constructed new noses) are briefly profiled. Information is presented using news capsules with first-person accounts, "interviews," letters to the editor, announcements, and some quaint advertisements for such miracle cures as live-ant wound closers and leeches, Roman baths, mechanical arms, and "fine flasks for super scientists." This rather elaborate and busy format, with full-color and black-and-white illustrations, easily catches a reader's interest. Gates provides a quick overview of the wonders and significant discoveries in the field of medicine. This title is more for browsing than research.

A time line is included.

Glossary: No
Bibliography: No
Index: Yes
Level: Beginning New Readers

Haughton, Emma. *Drinking, Smoking, and Other Drugs.*
Austin, TX: Raintree Steck-Vaughn, 2000.

Pages: 48
Series: Health and Fitness

This brief look at drugs begins with a definition of what they are, touching on drugs in history, where they come from, legal and illegal substances, and ways they are controlled. Subsequent chapters focus on alcohol, smoking, illegal drugs, medicinal drugs, avoiding the risks of addiction, and being sensible about using all drugs, including medicines. Sidebars contain additional information, including charts, diagrams, and some statistical data on the legal status of certain substances in the United States and Great Britain, worldwide smoking rates, heroin/crack addiction, and drug deaths. Captioned color photo illustrations fill the pages. Houghton's discussion of the consequences of addiction and how they can harm or help users is, to her credit, not preachy. This is a useful source of information for adults as a quick reference source and for educating children.

Glossary: Yes
Bibliography: Yes, of books, organizations, and Web sites
Index: Yes
Level: Beginning–Advanced New Readers

Hyde, Margaret. *Know About Drugs,* 4th ed. New York: Walker, 1995.

Pages: 93
Series: Know About

This short book is a quick guide to legal and illegal drugs. A general definition of drugs is followed by information on alcohol, nicotine, marijuana, PCP (phencyclidine) and other hallucinogens, inhalants, heroin, barbiturates, tranquilizers, crack/cocaine, ice, crystal, and steroids. The purpose of the book is to provide young readers with a vivid lesson on the serious physical effects of drugs and to discuss ways of preventing drug abuse by saying no and by getting high on life without drugs. The anti-drug pitch may inspire adult readers to make appropriate decisions for themselves and their children.

Glossary: No
Bibliography: No
Index: Yes
Level: Intermediate–Advanced New Readers

Macnair, Patricia. *Brain Power: The Brain, Nervous System, and Senses.* Boston: Kingfisher, 2005.

Pages: 40
Series: Bodyscope

Macnair sketches the anatomy and physiology of the brain in two-page chapters covering the central nervous system (brain, spinal cord, nervous system), reflexes, spinal injuries, the senses, consciousness, hormones, and control of the body (mind over matter). Each section has a brief introductory paragraph, brief generalized text, large color photos, diagrams, and text boxes containing snippets of related facts. Although colorful and quite generalized, the book is useful for readers in need of a simple explication of a complex subject.

Glossary: Yes
Bibliography: Yes, of Web sites
Index: Yes
Level: Beginning New Reader

Parker, Steve. *Medicine.* New York: DK, 2000.

Pages: 64
Series: Eyewitness

This remarkably detailed look at the history of medicine and the evolution of healing practices defines medicine, with discussion moving from the earliest evidence of its existence, including the contributions of Eastern philosophies, ancient Greece, the Roman Empire, Islamic traditions, and the Renaissance, to the development of modern medical practices. There are brief summaries of medical fads and fashions, natural medicines, modern drugs, some major alternative treatments, the history of psychiatry, surgical practices, prostheses, emergency medicine, the nature of general practice, the role of technology in medicine, and the future of medical practice.

The author includes statements on the inequality of medical care and the promise of modern research to discover successful treatments for currently incurable diseases. Biographical sketches and pictures of notable figures in the history of medicine are included. Each section, presented in double-page spreads, contains introductory text in large print followed by numerous vivid captioned illustrations with accurate labels. This visually and factually rich guide serves as an excellent ready-reference source for adults at any reading level.

Glossary: No
Bibliography: No
Index: Yes
Level: Beginning–Advanced New Readers

Parker, Steve. *Reproduction.* Chicago: Raintree, 2004.

Pages: 48
Series: Our Bodies

A short introduction defines the reproductive system common to each living thing, the stages of reproduction from intercourse to birth, and different views about reproduction. Sections on the female and male reproductive organs, the reproductive process, and growing up include double-page chapters, concisely and clearly written, along with attractive photos, detailed and labeled diagrams, and magnified photos from microscope slides. Topics include egg and sperm reproduction, the early embryo, life support in the uterus, the day of birth, the child, and child to adult development. Two sections discuss reproductive and birth problems. Color "Micro Body" boxes provide additional information on the uterine lining and the ripe egg cell. "Animal versus Human" color boxes and "Top Tips" provide supplemental information. Parker presents accurate data clearly and concisely. The book serves as a quick and simple introduction to the subject.

Glossary: Yes, of words appearing in boldface within the text
Bibliography: Yes, including two organizations
Index: Yes
Level: Beginning New Readers

Parramon, Merce. *Miracle of Life.* New York: Chelsea House, 1994.

Pages: 32
Series: Invisible World

An adult seeking a quick explanation of the process of human reproduction will likely be more than satisfied with this title. Non-technical text and striking color illustrations combine to depict simply and clearly the first step of the reproductive process, the female and male reproductive systems, body changes during puberty, how ova and sperm are formed, the development of the fetus and the placenta, the factors that determine the sex of the embryo. The laws of heredity are discussed in section "How We Develop."

Glossary: Yes
Bibliography: No
Index: Yes
Level: Beginning New Readers

Pringle, Laurence. *Smoking: A Risky Business.* New York: Morrow, 1996.

Pages: 128
Series: Save the Earth

Yes! At a time when the adult death and illness figures are rising and the tobacco industry is focusing on young people as a new primary source for profits, this book presents a succinct discussion of the harmful effects of a killer product. A brief history of tobacco products and their use precedes chapters on the mind-altering powers of nicotine; the rate of cigarette consumption in the United States; the antismoking movement and its advertising efforts; the negative effects of passive smoke on fetuses, infants, children, and adults; advertising methods used to hook new smokers; legal steps taken to stop cigarette advertisers from making such connections as sports and cigarettes, popularity and smoking, and beauty and smoking that appeal directly to young people; and citizen, business, and government movements to create a smoke-free society. The final chapter discusses how one can stop smoking or, better yet, never start. Photographs, reproductions of advertisements for and against smoking, and statistical charts enhance the text. This is an objective, nonpreachy presentation of the facts.

Glossary: Yes
Bibliography: Yes
Index: Yes
Level: Intermediate–Advanced New Readers

Ripoll, Jamie. *How Our Senses Work.* New York: Chelsea House, 1994.

Pages: 32
Series: Invisible World

A perfect blend of clear full-color illustrations and concise, easily readable text makes this picture book of how the senses work excellent for adults seeking basic information. Exactly how each of the five senses gathers the information that is sent to the brain to be processed is described. The sense centers in the brain are located in a color-coded drawing. The various chapters examine the anatomies of the eye, ear, nose, and skin and explain how each organ functions to produce sensory experiences. Four simple experiments for young readers are interesting enough to make some adults curious.

Glossary: Yes
Bibliography: No
Index: Yes
Level: Beginning New Readers

Simon, Seymour. *Eyes and Ears.* New York: HarperCollins, 2003.

Pages: Unpaginated
Series: —

With simple, direct writing, Simon clearly explains the structures and functions of the eyes and ears—how the eyes sense light and the ears sense sound, how they send nerve signals to the brain, and how the brain puts the information together. Also included are data on blind spots and the rod and cone shaped nerve cells in the retina, some examples of optical illusions, and information on how the semicircular canals of the ear affect balance. Clear diagrams and striking close-up color photos complement the text. This title is an accurate, succinct overview by a science writer well known for his ability to present basic facts against a background of amazing illustrations. This book serves as a good reference source for adults.

Glossary: No
Bibliography: No
Index: No
Level: Beginning New Readers

Walker, Richard. *Encyclopedia of the Human Body.* New York: DK, 2002.

Pages: 304
Series: —

This marvelously illustrated encyclopedia is divided into five categories: Working Parts, Moving Framework, Control and Sensation, Supply and Maintenance, and New Generations. The many double-page spreads within these categories give the reader a thorough, up-close look at many aspects of the human body—from its cells and DNA to the twenty-first-century study of genetics and the human genome project begun in 2000. A wealth of factual information is accessible via introductory paragraphs, concise definitions and explanations, detailed captioned photos, diagrams, charts, scans, and tables. Biographical data about some scientists are linked to the subjects discussed and appear in highlighted boxes. Such topics as disease, genetics, senses, blood, nutrition, stages of life, early man, the history of medicine, and alternative medicine are also covered. Running heads provide quick access to particular sections. A time line completes the book. This excellent, very readable, and comprehensive reference book on a high-interest topic is a good source for adults as well as young people.

Glossary: Yes
Bibliography: No

Index: Yes, with page numbers in boldface indicating the main reference to subjects and page numbers with the suffix "g" indicating a glossary entry
Level: Intermediate–Advanced New Readers

Wiltshire, Paula. *Dyslexia.* Austin, TX: Raintree Steck-Vaughn, 2003.

Pages: 64
Series: Health Issues

Wiltshire begins her book with a definition of dyslexia—a learning disability that affects between 8 and 10 percent of the population of the Western world—and a list of myths and truths about dyslexia. This compact book covers causes, diagnoses, effects of the condition (such as on memory and math), evaluation, and treatments. Case studies, captioned color photographs, and sidebars add to the book's usefulness. It serves as a quick reference.

Glossary: Yes
Bibliography: Yes, of books, organizations, and Web sites
Index: Yes
Level: Beginning New Readers

❊ Nature and ❊ Natural History

Arnold, Caroline. *Bat.* Photographs by Richard Hewett. New York: Morrow, 1996.

Pages: 48
Series: —

Exceptional full-color photographs and concise, easily understood text are combined to create a marvelous study of the bat. The author states that because many people do not know much about these creatures, they are underappreciated. She discounts superstitions and false ideas about bats. They do not attack humans or animals; they are not rabies carriers; they do not try to get tangled in one's hair. Bat history, anatomy, development, behavior, food, habitat, and predators are discussed. A section on endangered bats (almost 40 percent of the North American bat species) lists reasons for their endangerment and some ways of preventing their destruction.

Note: Many librarians also recommend *Bats: Wings in the Night,* by Patricia Lauber (New York: Random House, 1968), for adults.

Glossary: No
Bibliography: No
Index: Yes
Level: Beginning–Intermediate New Readers

Bash, Barbara. *Urban Roosts: Where Birds Nest in the City.*
Boston: Little, Brown, 1992.

Pages: 32
Series: —

An easy-to-read text with effective watercolor paintings done by the author, this title provides insight into why certain birds find homes in and around cities and thrive in a seemingly hostile environment. This picture book contains sufficient information to answer questions about a subject that generates much curiosity and controversy.

Glossary: No
Bibliography: No
Index: No
Level: Beginning

Bennett, Paul. *Pollinating a Flower.* New York: Raintree, 1994.

Pages: 32
Series: Nature's Secrets

Close-up photographs help define the scientific terms and concepts provided in the text. This picture book clearly discusses the importance of flowers as producers of seeds to make new plants and explains the process of pollination, including self-pollination and pollination by insects, by the wind, by birds, by some bats, by the Australian honey possum, by a South African rock mouse, and by some large animals like the red howler monkey. The concluding chapter briefly defines the term *botanist* and explains that artificial pollination is used to produce larger crops and disease-resistant plants, as well as different varieties of flowers. Two projects, clearly meant for young readers, are not so simplistic as to insult adults. They may even be of interest to those with a botanical bent. An enjoyable introduction to the subject, the book is useful to beginning adult readers.

Glossary: Yes
Bibliography: Yes
Index: Yes
Level: Beginning New Readers

Burnie, David. *Bird.* New York: DK, 2004.

Pages: 72
Series: Eyewitness

This pocket-sized guide is designed to help the reader notice and understand birds living around the home and community in urban, suburban, and rural areas. Specific birds, such as the house sparrow, starling, kestrel, pigeon, barn owl, seagull, duck, goose, humming-bird, and peregrine falcon, are used to illustrate and define birds in general. Their anatomy, different flight patterns, mating habits, reproduction, parenting, nesting and nesting materials, egg-hatching, first flights of chicks, bathing and preening activities, diet, and territorial habits are explored. Essential facts about bird habitats are clearly presented.

There are brief instructions (obviously meant for young readers) on preparing and dressing for bird watching, constructing an in-ground bird bath, and feeding birds. The text is supported by attractive color illustrations on every page, including the index. Although aimed at encouraging an interest in birds in young readers, this title serves as a handy source of information on the subject for adults. The back of the book shows that it is aimed at a young audience, and three illustrations depict a young child, but this should not discourage adults from using it.

Note: A few librarians recommend the related title, *Urban Roosts: Where Birds Nest in the City,* by Barbara Bash (San Francisco: Sierra Club Books/Boston: Little, Brown, 1992).

Glossary: No
Bibliography: No
Index: Yes
Level: Intermediate–Advanced New Readers

Burnie, David. The Kingfisher Illustrated Nature Encyclopedia. Boston: Kingfisher, 2004.

Pages: 320
Series: Kingfisher Encyclopedia Series

This guide to the many groups of animals and plants in the world, from microscopic single-celled organisms to giant redwoods and blue whales, begins with "A Plant Apart," a section that takes the reader through the formation of the earth, the beginning of life, and the evolution of life and the plants and animals extant, including information on survival, extinction, and rescue from extinction. Part 2, "The Living World," defines and explains the kingdoms of life—microlife, fungi, plants, and animals. It includes a discussion of ecology. "Wildlife Habitats," Part 3, describes such habitats as the arctic and tundra, deserts, grasslands, temperate, coniferous and tropical forests, mountains, oceans, and more. Special profile boxes focus on fascinating plants and animals like the Arctic bumblebee, the Antarctic cod, the California quail, vampire squid, Reindeer moss, and the welwitschia plant. Beautifully detailed and captioned color photographs (some double-page spreads) and clear diagrams make this an impressive reference source as well as a book for browsing.

Glossary: Yes
Bibliography: Yes, of Web sites
Index: Yes
Level: Advanced New Readers

Chrisp, Peter. The Whalers. New York: Raintree, 1995.

Pages: 48
Series: Remarkable World

This history of whaling begins with the first whalers, the Arctic Inuit, who hunted the bowhead whale while treating it with respect and killing it only to fill their needs for food, light, heat, and building materials. The emergence of commercial whaling, particularly to hunt the sperm whale for its oil, and the twentieth-century struggle to end commercial whaling and save the various species from extinction are then discussed. The description of life aboard a nineteenth-century whaling ship is equivalent to a visit to the New Bedford Whaling Museum in Massachusetts. The music, storytelling, work chanties, horrid food, sighting the whale, harpooning, the dangers of whaling, the Nantucket sleigh ride (the wounded whale dragging the whaleboat), the kill, the cutting-in and trying-out (boiling the blubber), and extracting and storing the oil are explained in words and pictures.

Sidebars provide related information on the reasons for hunting whales, the design of an American whaling ship, a sample sea chanty, background on Melville's writing of *Moby Dick*, and more. The illustrations, maps, and diagrams complement the text. Color pictures show what various whales look like. A time line is included. This book is a worthwhile source of information on all aspects of the subject.

Glossary: Yes, brief, because many terms are defined within the text
Bibliography: Yes, of five books, two videos, and a reference to the
    New Bedford Whaling Museum for further information
Index: Yes
Level: Beginning–Intermediate New Readers

Cosgrove, Brian. *Weather.* New York: DK, 2000.

Pages: 64
Series: Eyewitness

A superb combination of brief text and detailed captions to high-quality illustrations filling double-page chapters that define and explain the various aspects of weather makes this title an excellent choice for those who want a comprehensive presentation of the subject. The first section looks at "the restless air"—the atmosphere and its lower layer, the swirling, perpetually moving troposphere that gives the earth its sunny days, warm and cold periods, and seasonal storms, from gentle spring rains to raging blizzards. The second section, "Natural Signs," talks about how weather is predicted based on close observation of the natural world, with mention of some predictions based on folklore and superstition. Subsequent sections look at the science of weather, watching and forecasting it, the power of the sun, frost and ice, water in the air, clouds, rain, fronts and lows, storms, winds, fogs and mists, weather on the plains, in the mountains and by the sea, changes in weather, instruments used in a home weather station, and more. Packed with fascinating information, this book will be hard to put down before the last page is read.

Glossary: No
Bibliography: No
Index: Yes
Level: Beginning–Advanced New Readers

Creasy, Rosalind. *Blue Potatoes, Orange Tomatoes.* **Illustrated** by Ruth Heller. San Francisco: Sierra Club, 2000.

Pages: 40
Series: Books for Children

Blue potatoes, orange tomatoes, yellow zucchini, red chard, purple string beans, multicolored radishes, red popping corn, and yellow watermelon are introduced in this unique organic gardening book. It gives detailed instructions on growing a crop of these eight colorful fruits and vegetables: locating the garden; obtaining and planting the seeds; and fertilizing, watering, weeding, and protecting the plants from pests. Recipes are given for dishes such as sunshine zucchini muffins, fancy red and green salad, confetti bean salad with homemade dressing, microwave popcorn, and rainbow fruit salad. Supplementary information includes a list of seed companies and facts about plants and gardening tools. Large, colorful, detailed illustrations add to the enjoyment of the book. The example of a child's handwritten letter to a seed company and a picture of a little boy planting a seedling can easily be ignored by adults interested in learning about organic gardening.

Glossary: No
Bibliography: No

Index: Yes
Level: Beginning New Readers

Dowden, Anne Ophelia Todd. *The Blossom on the Bough: A Book of Trees.* Collingdale, PA: DIANE Publishing, 1999.

Pages: 71
Series: —

Originally published in 1975, this reprint is a memorable celebration of trees. Exquisitely illustrated with precise and inspired botanical drawings, the text is filled with adult-level scientific information blended with the author's expression of her deep personal appreciation of trees as majestic symbols of everlasting life, as seen in their cycle of life (new buds, blossoms, leaves, seeds) and death (coloring and dropping of leaves followed by a pseudo-death, or dormancy). Trees, such as the California sequoia, are among the oldest living things on earth. While these giants exist to be appreciated, other tree varieties have an important and intimate connection to human life. They provide fire for warmth, shelter, food and medicine, clothing, furniture, paper, and countless other things. The damage done by deforestation and pollution is emphasized.

Getting down to botanical matters, the author explains that trees are flowering plants. This is demonstrated through the unusual comparison of a sycamore to a buttercup. The growth cycle, the processes of photosynthesis and pollination, the development of fruits and seeds, and the process of vegetative reproduction are clearly explained. The illustrations of each tree's blossoms, seeds, and leaves might be used as a tree identification guide. A map showing the forest regions of the country is followed by a list of the common trees found in the different areas of the United States. An outstanding, thought-provoking introduction to the blossoms, fruits, and seeds on the boughs of deciduous and evergreen trees in this country, the book has definite appeal for all ages.

Glossary: No
Bibliography: No

Index: Yes, with page references to the illustrations in italic
Level: Beginning–Advanced New Readers

Downs, Sandra. *Shaping the Earth: Erosion.* Brookfield, CT:
Twenty-First Century Books, 2000.

Pages: 64
Series: Exploring Planet Earth

Downs begins with a definition of erosion—the slow process of
breaking down and carrying away rocks to recycle the earth's surface
and create mineral-rich soil. Along with mechanical and chemical
weathering, erosion deposits materials in new places. The chapters
are devoted to erosion by rain, running water, ocean waves beating
against shores, glaciers, wind, and, finally, human activity (with the
potential to speed up the process). The captioned, color photo illustrations provide excellent examples of the erosion by the different
elements described. Highlighted boxes, with small photos, provide
added information on such topics as shape shifting (natural bridge in
Virginia), rain forest "vitamins" (mineral-rich clay in Manu National
Park, Peru), floods and farming (flooding in Bangladesh), glacial
sculptures (Garden Wall, Glacier National Park, Montana), and more.
Downs's writing style is descriptive and absorbing. The book
provides a fascinating overview of the subject.

Glossary: Yes
Bibliography: Yes, of books, Web sites, and places to visit
Index: Yes
Level: Intermediate New Readers

**Grassy, John and Chuck Keene. *National Audubon Society First
Field Guide: Mammals.*** New York: Scholastic, 1998.

Pages: 159
Series: Audubon Society First Field Guide

The book begins with an explanation of what a naturalist is, citing L.
David Meech, a mammalologist who studies wolves, and Lewis and

Clark, self-taught naturalists, and includes the rules for mammal watching. The first section, "The World of Mammals," looks at different kinds—land-roving, airborne, underground, and seafaring: their habitats, bodies, senses, foods, survival skills, and social lives. One section describes the signs of their activities (tracks, trails, etc.), and one explains how to use the field guide. Then follows a list of 50 common North American mammals and 79 of their look-alikes. Each two-page spread has a large photo of the animal in its native habitat, a brief paragraph of information, and a description of its markings, size, signs (tracks and droppings), habitat, and geographical range. There are smaller photos of the look-alikes plus brief facts on them. A metric conversion chart is included. An attractive colorful beginning guide, this book is also suitable for adult ready-reference use.

Glossary: Yes
Bibliography: Yes, of books, tapes and disks, Web sites,
    and organizations
Index: Yes
Level: Intermediate–Advanced New Readers

Green, Jen. *Rainforest Revealed.* New York: DK, 2004.

Pages: 38
Series: DK Revealed

This well-researched title takes the reader on a tour of the lush habitats of different types of rainforests—tropical and temperate forests, cloud forests, flood forests, and mangrove swamps. A double-page spread introduces each type with a brief informative paragraph in large type, a map of locations in the world, and short descriptions. Subsequent chapters look at the plant and animal life in the tree tops, on the forest floor, and on the ground and then discuss the trees and plants that sustain the forest, plant reproduction, the food web, the Amazon rainforest, how animal life gets around, prey and predators, mating, nocturnal animals, the ancient Mayan ruins of Palenque and the Temple of the Sun, the people of the rainforests, and, finally, the destruction of the forests and steps taken to preserve them.

Magnificent color photos (some with acetate pages providing multidimensional views) are striking. Written by an expert in the field, the book is an excellent introduction to the subject and perfect for browsing.

Glossary: No
Bibliography: No
Index: Yes
Level: Beginning New Readers

Horton, Casey. *Parrots.* Tarrytown, NY: Benchmark, 1996.

Pages: 32
Series: Endangered!

Parrots are colorful, popular pets with the ability to talk and do all sorts of tricks. Without question, trapping and smuggling them for the pet trade is the major reason some of the more than 300 parrot species have either become extinct or are endangered. Other reasons for their disappearance are the destruction of their habitat and trapping or shooting them for sport.

Striking color photographs accompany brief descriptions of a few endangered parrots. These include the scarlet macaw, found in Central and South America; the kea parrots and the flightless kakapo of New Zealand; the thick-billed parrots of Mexico and the United States; and the St. Lucia parrots. The author briefly describes their physical appearance, living habits, and the reasons they are endangered. Maps show where the birds are found, and organizations that provide more information about parrots and how people can help protect them are listed. This poignant nutshell view of what humans are doing to destroy these exquisite birds and the actions that must be taken to help them survive presents a strong argument for conservation.

Glossary: Yes
Bibliography: Yes
Index: Yes
Level: Beginning New Readers

Kramer, Stephen. *Caves.* Photographs by Kenrick L. Day.
Minneapolis: Carolrhoda, 1995.

Pages: 48
Series: Nature in Action

Beautifully descriptive prose begins on a black page that symbolizes
the darkness and absolute silence of an unexplored cave, the wonders
of which were created over thousands of years by the endless drip-
ping of water. The time of discovery comes when a flashlight beam
reveals the beauty created by the water. Marvelous photographs and
a map of the limestone regions of the world make the caves come
alive. The book contains the definition of a cave and discusses types
of caves, how they are formed, how speleothems (stone shapes, such
as stalactites, stalagmites, and helictites) are created, cave plant and
animal life, human exploration, and the use of caves. Rules of cave
safety and how caves are protected from damage precede some
fascinating facts about caves. The scientific terms are clearly defined
and easily understood by new adult readers. The amount of information contained in the text, along with the photographs, might
attract adults with more than basic reading skills.

Glossary: Yes
Bibliography: No
Index: Yes
Level: Beginning–Intermediate New Readers

Kramer, Stephen. *Lightning.* Minneapolis: Carolrhoda, 1993.

Pages: 48
Series: Nature in Action

Dramatic photographs, along with some beautiful full-color illustrations, support the text on each page of this presentation of a wide
variety of facts about lightning. The book fulfills any adult's need for
concisely stated information on how lightening is formed, what
happens when it strikes, the methods used by scientists to study it,
definitions of the different kinds of lightning, the role thunder plays

in a lightning storm, the kinds of clouds that make lightning, and safety tips on how to avoid injury by lightning. A color-coded map of the average number of thunderstorm days in a year answers the question of whether or not lightning occurs all over the world with the same frequency. Some myths and additional facts presented include the Greek belief that the places lightning strikes are sacred and the facts that airplanes hit by lightning usually keep flying; the gases heated by lightning mix with rain and fall to the earth as natural fertilizer while the gas called ozone rises into the atmosphere to protect the earth from the sun's harmful rays; lightning really does strike twice; and a flash of lightning is hot enough to melt sand. Despite one easily ignored reminder that this is a children's book (that an adult should unplug TVs, stereos, and computers for safety during a thunderstorm), *Lightning* can be used effectively by adults at any reading level.

Glossary: Yes
Bibliography: No
Index: No
Level: Beginning–Intermediate New Readers

Lauber, Patricia. *News About Dinosaurs.* Madison, WI: Turtleback, 1994.

Pages: 48
Series: —

Here is a dinosaur book with a different slant. The author provides background on long-standing scientific theories and beliefs, announces the news about the latest discoveries, and discusses how they changed scientific thinking and how theories are revised as research continues. The drawings and paintings, and their captions, serve to clarify the textual presentation. A pronounciation guide and an index are quite useful to the reader.

Other dinosaur books by Lauber are also excellent sources of information: *Dinosaurs Walked Here and Other Stories Fossils Tell* (New York: Bradbury, 1987: 56 pages); *Living with Dinosaurs* (New York:

Bradbury, 1991: 48 pages); and *How Dinosaurs Came to Be* (New York: Simon & Schuster Books for Young Readers, 1996: 48 pages).

Glossary: No
Bibliography: No
Index: Yes, with page references to illustrations in boldface
Level: Beginning New Readers

Lippincott, Kristen. *Astronomy.* New York: DK, 2004.

Pages: 72
Series: Eyewitness

The reader is led through an investigation of many aspects of astronomy, including the definition and meaning of the term; various developments in the history of ancient astronomy; the ordering of the universe; how astronomy and astrology are practiced; the Copernican revolution; the contributions of Galileo and Newton; the history of the invention of the telescope; a brief discussion of observatories; and space exploration. Following sections explore the solar system—the sun, moon, earth, and all the planets. Finally, there are chapters on comets, asteroids, and meteorites; on the birth and death of stars; and on the exploration of galaxies and the universe beyond. Brief biographies and pictures of significant astronomers are included. The chapters (in two-page spreads) are filled with clearly labeled pictures, charts, and cutaways. This fact-filled book serves as an excellent primary reference source for all ages.

Glossary: No
Bibliography: No
Index: Yes
Level: Beginning–Intermediate New Readers

Mattson, Mark T. *Scholastic Environmental Atlas of the United States.* New York: Scholastic, 1993.

Pages: 80
Series: —

Maps, graphs, charts, diagrams, and photographs support a text about various aspects of the U.S. environment, how humans have adversely affected our part of the planet, and what can be done to restore the balance of nature by working toward correcting pollution-related problems and preventing further damage. The first chapter defines ecosystems. Subsequent discussions concern people, forests, farms, cities and suburbs, garbage, and air and water resources. The author looks at the portion of global natural resources consumed in the United States (the greatest amount) and how its citizens can conserve energy and prevent pollution. Each chapter has a "focus" page on a topic related to the material covered. There are statistical facts on the United States and each state (compiled from the 1990 census and the 1980 and 1992 *World Almanac*), a list of organizations to write to for information on the environment, and projects developed for children, which can be bypassed by adult readers. This is an easy book on a high-interest topic with much solid information.

Glossary: Yes
Bibliography: Yes, arranged by subject
Index: Yes
Level: Intermediate New Readers

McClish, Bruce. *Earth's Continents.* Chicago: Heinemann, 2003.

Pages: 32
Series: —

This book opens with a definition of a continent and goes on to discuss the early scientists' belief that continents were fixed and the modern discovery, based on fossil studies, that they moved great distances in ancient times. The author also looks at the effect this movement of continents had on the creation of mountains, valleys, oceans, currents, the weather and where animals, plants, and people chose to live. Also covered are topics such as the making of a continent, continental drift, continental landscapes, climate and wildlife, and relationships among continents. Captioned and labeled illustrations and maps, along with a fact box in each chapter, clarify the text. This brief look at continents is a solid quick reference source for adults.

Glossary: Yes
Bibliography: Yes
Index: Yes
Level: Beginning New Reader

Ricciuti, Edward R. and the National Audubon Society Staff.
National Audubon Society First Field Guide: Rocks and Minerals.
New York: Barnes & Noble, 2005.

Pages: 160
Series: Audubon Society First Field Guide

This excellent introductory field guide to rocks and minerals begins with a discussion of basic geology and mineralogy—defining a geologist, a mineral, a rock and the three classes of rock (igneous, sedimentary, and metamorphic), and volcanoes in brief text and impressive color photographs with informative captions. The second part of the book includes information about identifying rocks and minerals—color, streak and luster, hardness and weight—and about gemstones, fossils, and the ages of rocks and minerals. The field guide section (Part 3) contains impressive color photographs of 50 significant rocks and minerals and boxed information on their properties, colors, and environment. Included with each entry are shorter descriptions of more than 120 related specimens. The reference section (Part 4) has a table of the minerals presented in the guide. This is a handy reference source also appropriate for adults.

Glossary: Yes, of technical terms used by geologists and naturalists
Bibliography: Yes, of books, organizations, and Web sites
Index: Yes
Level: Intermediate–Advanced New Readers

Ridpath, Ian. *Facts on File Stars and Planets Atlas: New Edition.*
New York: Facts on File, 2005.

Pages: 80
Series: Facts on File Atlas

This remarkable, all-inclusive, up-to-date guide to the stars and planets is written in precise and easy language and enriched by captioned full-color illustrations derived from data gathered by recent space probes and pictures taken by the Hubble telescope. Chapters cover the solar system, sun, earth, moon, eclipses and tides, individual planets, comets, asteroids, meteors and meteorites, stars and constellations, star charts, navigation by the stars, birth of stars, supernova, star families, our galaxy, other galaxies and the universe, the origin of the universe, telescopes and binoculars, and seeing the invisible. Diagrams illustrate the distances of the planets from the sun, fusion reactions that power the sun, the seasons caused by the tilting of the earth's axis, phases of the moon, the tides, how eclipses happen, the changing shapes of constellations, the orbit of a pair of stars, and how three main types of telescopes work. Data boxes highlighted in pink are given for the sun, earth, moon, and each of the planets. Pictures of postage stamps commemorating space exploration and discoveries appear throughout the text.

Glossary: No
Bibliography: No
Index: Yes
Level: Beginning–Intermediate New Readers

Taylor, Barbara. *Butterflies and Moths.* New York: DK, 2004.

Pages: 160
Series: Pocket Guides

A title in a new series of pocket books, this reference guide to the world of butterflies and moths is jam-packed with facts. The introductory section provides data on the wide variety of shapes and sizes of these insects, their life cycles, various ways of distinguishing a butterfly from a moth, the reasons for the many colors, the structure of the wings and flight patterns, the significance of their senses and how the senses are developed and used, how and what they eat and drink, the mating process, caterpillar growth and change, migration and hibernation, and the effects of environmental change on their habitats. Following sections discuss the butterflies and moths that live in tropical rain forests, wetlands, grasslands and barrens, dry regions and caves, and in arctic and mountain regions and give some examples of species in these habitats. A reference section provides a handy guide to classification; some amazing lifestyle and behavior facts; a list of threatened habitats, with information on what the threats are and which species are at risk; information on where to look for the insects in order to study them, how to observe and record those seen, and the equipment needed; and instructions on how to rear them from eggs and how to create a butterfly garden by growing plants that will attract them.

The mini-illustrations are precise and remarkably clear, considering their size. Each is nicely labeled, and captions and annotations provide further clarification. Running page headings clearly identify each subject and section of the book. Numerous fact boxes contain additional information. With the exception of the cataloging-in-publication data and the fact that it is shelved in the children's collection, there is no evidence that this title is juvenile literature.

Glossary: Yes, of the more technical terms used
Bibliography: No, but a selected list of worldwide organizations
Index: Yes, a subject index and an index of common scientific
    names
Level: Intermediate–Advanced New Readers

Turner, Alan. *National Geographic Prehistoric Mammals.*
Illustrated by Mauricio Anton. Washington, DC: National
Geographic, 2004.

Pages: 192
Series: —

This fascinating study of mammalian history goes beyond the age of dinosaurs to include a wide range of extinct mammals, from whales to rodents, from bats to Neanderthals. Each section, divided by order and species, contains representative beasts, a time line, fact box, global distribution map, and some indication of scale—usually a silhouette of a modern-day six foot *Homo sapiens* drawn to the same scale or, in the case of smaller mammals, just the foot. Eye-catching full-color illustrations enrich the concise, informative text.

A brief general introduction touches on the exciting changes in the study of prehistoric mammals through technological advances in the analysis of fossil evidence. A number of introductory spreads follow—discussion of the ages of mammals, reconstructions from fossils, behavior, classification, and an explanation of the features of the profiles presented in the body of the book. This title is a high-quality resource on the link between modern animals and their prehistoric predecessors for quick reference, as well as for browsing.

Glossary: Yes
Bibliography: No, but a list of national and local museums in
    foreign countries and in the United States
Index: Yes
Level: Intermediate–Advanced New Readers

Twist, Clint. *1000 Facts on Oceans.* New York: Barnes & Noble, 2005.

Pages: 223
Series: 1000 Facts

This book is a concise guide to ocean features, amazing life forms, and feats of exploration. The information, presented in 1,000 bulleted points, ranges from underwater volcanoes and sea caves through submersibles and coral reefs. The facts are clearly highlighted with color images and diagrams and informative captions. The contents includes sections on sea and coast, marine fish, mammals, birds and reptiles, history and exploration, ships and boats, the human impact on oceans, early marine life, fish facts, seahorses and sharks, the blue planet and oceans, volcanic oceans, glaciers, whales, penguins, first boats to use modern navigation, fossil fuels, and living at sea. There are fact boxes on various subjects, including Christopher Columbus, "Finding the Way" (navigation), and "Oceans in Danger" (pollution). The book provides a quick overview of topics related to oceans that is a good source for browsing while building a background knowledge of oceans.

Glossary: No
Bibliography: No
Index: Yes
Level: Intermediate–Advanced New Readers

Vogt, Gregory L. *Earth*. Minneapolis: Lerner, 1996.

Pages: 32
Series: Gateway Solar System

The author, a member of the staff of NASA's Education Division at the Johnson Space Center in Houston, Texas, works with astronauts to develop educational videos for schools. This fact-packed book, the next best source to a video, beautifully illustrates earth's fragility and majesty in images captured from space. The well-written descriptive text and NASA photographs show the amount of plant life in different areas of the earth, how the continents once fit together like a giant jigsaw puzzle, the relationship of the moon to the earth, the makeup of the moon, and more. The book contains a page of quick facts about Earth, including the derivation of its name. The book is an excellent source of current information from NASA, and its format and large print make it an easy title to read. The technical terms are clearly defined as well. Adult beginning and intermediate readers will find this source an enjoyable introduction to our planet.

Glossary: Yes, the terms included appear in italic throughout the
    text
Bibliography: Yes
Index: Yes
Level: Beginning New Readers

Walker, Jane. *Avalanches and Landslides.* Mankato, MN: Stargazer Books, 2005.

Pages: 32
Series: Natural Disasters

A brief introduction describes the impact of avalanches and landslides: "they strike quickly, often without warning, and . . . can be catastrophic, crushing to death or burying alive people and animals, and whatever else lies within the path." The author points out that, despite improved warning systems that help minimize loss of life, humans must attempt to prevent triggering these disasters. Double-page chapters define avalanches and landslides and focus on particular disasters in history, dating back to ancient times, and then examines what can be done to reduce activities people engage in that cause avalanches and landslides.

The text is rich with effective photo illustrations and cutaways that are remarkable for their clarity. A fact file provides brief data on the world's largest landslides, recent disasters (1990–2003), avalanche control in Canada, mudflow technology, and mining waste disasters. This brief overview provides adult readers with concise definitions and explanations on the subject, as well as a place to start for more in-depth research.

Glossary: Yes
Bibliography: No
Index: Yes
Level: Beginning–Intermediate New Readers

Walker, Richard. *Dinosaurs.* New York: St. Martin's Press, 2000.

Pages: 58
Series: Golden Photo Guide

The next best thing to a museum tour, this modest book combines brief factual text with impressive photo illustrations and informative captions to provide a concise look at dinosaurs. The double-page sections define dinosaurs; touch on the first of these extraordinary reptiles and on the Jurassic and Cretaceous periods; describe the bodies and structures of the different parts of the bodies of dinosaurs; and explore how they lived, moved, kept warm, hunted, defended themselves, reproduced, and more.

The fossil hunt and formal study of extinct giant reptiles began in 1841, and they were named dinosaurs (meaning "terrible lizards") by Sir Richard Owen (1804–1892). The section on the discovery of dinosaurs is followed by a look at dinosaur fossils and how the structures of dinosaurs are re-created, the evolution of modern birds from small theropods, and theories of extinction. This title is ideal for those in need of brief facts on the subject.

Glossary: No
Bibliography: No
Index: Yes
Level: Intermediate New Readers

Weindensaul, Scott. *National Audubon Society First Field Guide: Birds.* New York: Barnes & Noble, 2005.

Pages: 160
Series: Audubon Society First Field Guide

An excellent introduction to birds, the book is divided into four parts. Part 1 introduces the world of birds—there are over 9,000 species, with about 650 of them (both nesting and migratory) living in North America. Covered here are taxonomy, bird anatomy, feathers, flight, migration, nesting, raising chicks, bird identification, color differences, body shapes, bills and beaks, wings and tails, why birds sing, and where they live. Part 2 provides a lesson in bird identification, including markings, colors, shapes, songs, bird ranges, and habitat, plus a bit on endangered species and organizations working to save them. Part 3, the field guide, provides descriptive details of 50 common North American birds, along with range maps and impressive color photographs beautifully laid out. For each of the 50 birds, the entry includes shorter descriptions of two or three birds in the same family, for example, Canada Goose: Snow Goose, Tundra

Swan. Part 4, the reference section, includes an illustrated list of the 50 state birds and their common names and a glossary of terms used by ornithologists, naturalists, and birders. There is also a list of photo and illustration credits. This modest volume is an excellent beginning birder book for adults.

Glossary: Yes
Bibliography: Yes, of books, tapes and disks, organizations, and
     Web sites
Index: Yes
Level: Intermediate–Advanced New Readers

❈ Pets and Pet Care ❈

Alderton, David. *Cats*. New York: DK, 2003.

Pages: 160
Series: DK Pockets

This book is a guide for anyone fascinated by cats or considering adopting one. The first chapter describes the evolution of cats and explains their anatomy and characteristic features. A general chapter on the coat lengths of particular breeds of cats is followed by illustrated guides to long-haired and short-haired cats that are extremely useful for selecting a cat as a pet. The world's wild cats are featured in the next chapter. A reference section contains information on cat classification, endangered cats, what to consider when choosing a cat, caring for a cat, common health problems, first aid, and how to understand a cat's body language. Two pages of amazing cat records contain facts about size, history, life span, feats, the most valuable cat, and more. A list of organizations to contact for information on cat health, pedigree standards and cat shows, fighting against animal cruelty, and the world's wild cats is included. Characteristic of this series, this comprehensive pocket reference guide is filled with vivid pictures, charts, lists, introductory text, captions, labels, headings, and annotations.

Glossary: Yes
Bibliography: No
Index: Yes.
Level: Intermediate–Advanced New Readers

Alderton, David. *Encyclopedia of Aquarium and Pond Fish.*
Photography by Max Gibbs. New York: DK, 2005.

Pages: 400
Series: —

This book provides comprehensive coverage of the species most commonly sold in aquarium stores, as well as some unusual species of fish, invertebrates, and plants—including both scientific and common names. Divided into three main sections, freshwater aquariums, marine aquariums, and ponds, the book offers practical advice on caring for fish, setting up the tank, feeding, checking health, treating illness, breeding, and caring for and maintaining the tank. A directory of species is organized by related groups.

The book begins with an introduction to fish keeping, the anatomy of a fish, evolution and classification, and a three-page section on the popularity of fish keeping. The fish directory entries provide data on origins, size, diet, water, temperament, all in boxed sections. In addition, there is descriptive text as well as color photos.

This title provides up-to-date expert information and guidance that is rich with marvelous high-quality color photos and quick reference sections. An outstanding reference source, the book is appropriate for both beginning and experienced enthusiasts.

Glossary: Yes
Bibliography: Yes, of Web sites
Index: Yes, of common and scientific names and a general index
Level: Advanced New Readers

Athan, Mattie Sue and Dianalee Deter-Townsend.
The Second-Hand Parrot. Hauppauge, NY: Barrons, 2002.

Pages: 95
Series: —

The parrot that has lived in one or more previous homes is more often than not thought to be a "damaged" bird with behavioral problems, including excessive screaming, biting, fearfulness, and feather plucking. These problems result from poor human guidance and assistance as well as inappropriate training from novices ignorant of parrot needs and proper care. With commitment, patience, and constant attention to the bird's needs, many second-hand parrots have the potential of being turned into a treasured pet, an ideal companion bird.

The authors discuss the kinds of birds available—wild-caught parrots, found birds, physically damaged or bereaved parrots, and more. The costs involved in new cages, toys, time for exercise, bathing, health care, nutrition, corrective grooming, acclimation, and behavior modification are explained. The text is supplemented with data on the life spans of companion parrots, a cage checklist, simple household items that can be used to encourage playing, and hazards in the home. Color photos with captions fill the pages of this informative book. The authors make a strong argument for adopting a displaced bird, and the reader is assured that these parrots can indeed make wonderful pets.

Glossary: Yes
Bibliography: Yes, of books, organizations, videos, and Web sites
Index: Yes
Level: Intermediate–Advanced New Readers

Bartlett, Richard D. and Patricia Bartlett. *Turtles and Tortoises.* Hauppauge, NY: Barron's, 2006.

Pages: 112
Series: —

This guide, rich with clear color photographs, covers the basics of turtles and tortoises as pets: their needs, care (housing, dietary requirements), making choices, and hand-rearing them. It identifies a healthy specimen and includes information on pond turtles and specialized aquatics. There are short descriptive pieces on the various species, including range, habits, appearance, and behavior. Various checklists and tip boxes are included. The all-important laws regarding the keeping of turtles are identified on page 39. This step-by-step guide to daily care, and more, serves as a basic handbook for novice turtle and tortoise enthusiasts.

Glossary: Yes
Bibliography: Yes, of clubs, books, and magazines
Index: Yes
Level: Intermediate–Advanced New Readers

Deutsch, Robin. *The Healthy Bird Cookbook: A Lifesaving Nutritional Guide and Recipe Collection.* Neptune City, NJ: T.F.H., 2004.

Pages: 192
Series: —

A balanced diet is as essential for birds as it is for humans. Part I discusses the need for more than just seed; the necessary food groups, vitamins, minerals, and amino acids; special diets; and the all-important foods to avoid and other hazards. Part II lists recipes for birds: breads and muffins, breakfast foods, eggs and omelettes, pastas and pizzas, rice and noodle dishes, sandwiches and wraps, beans and seed mixes, vegetable dishes, fruits, desserts, snacks, mashes, and meats.

If you think it's crazy to cook for your bird, think about cooking a meal for the both of you. Try a polly pizza, a sweet potato muffin, or a birdie omelette. Delicious! Filled with vital information and easy-to-follow recipes, this title is a valuable resource guide to a healthy diet.

Glossary: No
Bibliography: Yes, of organizations, publications, Internet
    resources, veterinary resources, emergency resources, and
    rescue organizations
Index: Yes
Level: Advanced New Readers

Edney, Andrew and David Taylor. *101 Essential Tips: Cat Care.*
New York: DK, 2003.

Pages: 72
Series: 101 Essential Tips

This brief, fact book is a good introduction to the world of cat ownership and cat care. It covers the how-tos of choosing a cat, housing, handling, feeding, grooming, health, first aid, and more. The text is enhanced by clear, captioned color photos, and the step-by-step information effectively provides quick answers to a wide variety of questions. This book is a handy basic manual.

Glossary: No
Bibliography: No
Index: Yes
Level: Intermediate New Readers

Eldridge, Wayne Bryant. *The Best Pet Name Book Ever!*,
3rd ed. Hauppauge, NY: Barron's, 2003.

Pages: 288
Series: —

This book lists more than 3,000 pet names categorized by subject areas, including personality, historical names, human names, foreign words and names, literature and art, cartoon characters, fashion and cosmetics, and pairs and trios. Black and white cartoons sprinkled throughout the text add a bit of humor. Based on the examples of a snake called Gucci, a parrot named Cleopas, Dubya the hound, and a goldfish named Courvoisier, readers are bound to find a name for a dog, cat, bird, goldfish, iguana, or any other type of pet.

Glossary: No
Bibliography: No
Index: No
Level: Beginning–Advanced New Readers

Evans, Jim. *What If My Dog . . . ?: Pulls . . . Won't Eat . . . Barks . . . Is Aggressive . . . Jumps Up . . . Is Shaking . . . Soiled the Rug . . . etc. . . . etc. . . . ? Expert Answers to All Those Doggie Problems.* Hauppauge, NY: Barron's, 2006.

Pages: 160
Series: —

This handy resource explains how to deal with a variety of problems a dog owner may experience, from excessive barking to aggressiveness to people and other dogs, chewing household furniture, suffering injury or a serious health problem, and more. The book is divided into four color-coded parts that cover understanding dog behavior and how it can be shaped; mishaps and problems around the house and outdoors; preventing and coping with illness, the aging dog, and maintaining quality of life; and the what-ifs. Each part begins with its own table of contents. The book is easy to use, filled with color photos, color and black-and-white illustrations, and humorous cartoons. Highlighted fact boxes provide additional information, such as how to interpret a dog's body language, training tips, helpful hints, dos and don'ts, safety tips, tips on keeping the dog fit, and tips on improving the dog's quality of life. Ease of use and concise, clear language make the book a pleasure to read.

Glossary: No
Bibliography: No
Index: Yes
Level: Intermediate–Advanced New Readers

Morton, E. Lynn. *Ferrets: Everything About Purchase, Care, Nutrition, Diseases, Behavior, and Breeding.* Hauppauge, NY: Barron's, 2000.

Pages: 95
Series: —

The author maintains that ferrets remain misunderstood, that they are pets just like cats and dogs, but many others disagree. In many localities and states these fur balls are considered wild animals and are forbidden as pets (i.e., New York City). Concise chapters cover selecting and purchasing decisions, supplies needed, handling, grooming, escaping and common accidents, training, feeding, health care, reproduction, and breeding. The book concludes with a section on understanding one's ferret—anatomy, intelligence and sense organs, social behavior, and play gestures—a brief history of ferrets, and some misconceptions about them. Useful boxed sections provide additional data: 10 tips for new ferret owners, how to protect furniture, disciplining the ferret, a list of common poisonous out-door plants, the dos and don'ts of ferret ownership, hidden home dangers, and a how-to on understanding this pet. Captioned color photographs and black-and-white illustrations complement the text. This basic first guide is well suited for adults.

Glossary: No
Bibliography: Yes, of useful addresses and Internet sites
Index: Yes
Level: Intermediate–Advanced New Readers

Pinney, Chris C. *The Complete Home Veterinary Guide,* 3rd ed. New York: McGraw Hill, 2004.

Pages: 820
Series: —

Filled with facts, instructions, and advice, this authoritative guide, authored by a veterinarian, provides quick answers on health care, health, diseases, training, first aid, and many other topics for people with one or more species in the household—from the most popular dogs, cats, and birds to gerbils, mice, rats, hedgehogs, miniature pot-bellied pigs, invertebrates, and tropical fish, to name a few. Part One contains 18 chapters on dogs and cats, including a history, how to choose the right pet, emergency first aid before bringing the animal to the vet, training, traveling with a dog or cat, preventive health care, elective surgeries, diseases, anatomy, and physiology.

Part Two, devoted to birds, examines factors to consider in choosing the right bird, explains avian anatomy and physiology, and looks at preventive health care, general treatment of sick birds, and avian diseases and disorders. Part Three discusses the basics of rabbits, guinea pigs, hamsters and gerbils, mice and rats, chinchillas, prairie dogs, hedgehogs, sugar gliders, and more. Part Four contains related topics—first aid for dogs and cats, caring for injured and orphaned wildlife, care of the older pet, increasing longevity, cancer in companion animals, holistic pet care, and strategies for reducing the cost of pet ownership.

The book includes an appendix of clinical signs and complaints in dogs and cats and one listing medications for dogs and cats. Fact boxes, vet tips, tables, "fact or fiction" boxes, and line drawings supplement the text. This title is to be used only as a reference guide, not to replace a visit to the vet. It is a clearly and concisely written first source for use prior to going to a species-specific book, if one is at hand.

Glossary: Yes
Bibliography: No
Index: Yes
Level: Intermediate–Advanced New Readers

Rach, Julie. *The Simple Guide to Bird Care and Training.*
Neptune City, NJ: T.F.H., 2002.

Pages: 224
Series: —

This practical guide begins with an all-important chapter on starting out: considering the pros and cons of living with a pet bird, what is involved with day-to-day care, the cost of pet bird ownership, where to acquire a bird, information on wild birds, and the history of bird keeping. Data boxes include questions to ask when purchasing a bird, a list of the top ten parrots for beginners, and a regional breakdown of parrot species. Chapter Two provides information on the various species and their characteristics, along with a small color picture of each one. Bringing the bird home is covered in Chapter 3, including bird handling, bird-proofing the home, household hazards, birds and children and with other pets, selecting a vet, and the settling-in time. Chapter 4 discusses the cage and accessories, its size and location, and the aviary as a housing alternative.

The second part of the book includes a comprehensive discussion of bird behavior—that which indicates illness, boredom, and stress (as opposed to normal behaviors). There are instructions on how to interpret body language, methods of socializing and bonding with the bird, and more. Feeding and nutrition, maintaining health, caring for older birds, grooming, training, and breeding are addressed in subsequent chapters. Rach's book is a "must read" for those considering a pet bird and for "first bird" people. It is chock-full of facts, tips, and explanations on all aspects of pet bird ownership and nicely complemented with fact boxes and captioned color photos.

Glossary: No
Bibliography: Yes, of periodicals, organizations, and bird clubs and societies
Index: Yes
Levels: Advanced New Readers

Sanford, Gina. *The Tropical Aquarium: Comprehensive Coverage, from Setting Up an Aquarium to Choosing the Best Fishes.* Hauppauge, NY: Barron's, 2004.

Pages: 208
Series: —

This title is a perfect quick reference guide and manual for those starting an aquarium. Clear, concise text, complemented by color photos and some diagrams and maps showing the origins of the fishes profiled, is presented in three parts: setting up the aquarium (step by step); options and continuing care and maintenance; and profiles of fish, listed by common and scientific names. Each entry has descriptive data, a list of ideal conditions, a map of the origin of the species, and special data concerning the individual species. This is a perfect reference source for the beginning hobbyist.

Glossary: No
Bibliography: No
Index: Yes
Level: Intermediate–Advanced New Readers

Seidensticker, John and Susan Lumpkin. *Smithsonian Q & A: Cats.* New York: HarperCollins, 2006.

Pages: 218
Series: Smithsonian Q & A

A descriptive look at the nature and wonder of cats, from tabbies to tigers, begins the book. The first chapter defines the domestic cat and the cat family in general. The origins of wild and domestic cats are then explored, and new and old breeds are identified. Genetic composition, with a gene chart, is included. Then follows a look at anatomy and how cats sense the world. Subsequent chapters discuss domestic cats as predators, their social life, and their body language. A ready-reference section describes the breeds, and the authors then take a look at males and females, kittens, birth and care, and growth and learning. Chapters on cats and people and wild cats end the book. Rich with captioned color photos, the Q & A format of this quick reference source makes it easy to use. It is an excellent information guide recommended for adults as well as young people.

Glossary: Yes
Bibliography: Yes
Index: Yes
Level: Intermediate–Advanced New Readers

Siegal, Mordecai and Matthew Margolis. *I Just Got a Puppy; What Do I Do?* New York: Fireside, 2002.

Pages: 202
Series: —

There is no need to stare at the fluffy pup in horror as he piddles on the Persian rug, chews up the new slippers, or whines loudly at two in the morning. This practical guide covers bonding with a puppy, feeding, training, and more. The training techniques are presented with illustrations—an asset for the novice. Profiles of the 25 most popular breeds are handy for the puppy selection process. This is an excellent quick-reference instruction manual to bring home with the new wiggling pet to quickly get things started in the right direction.

Glossary: No
Bibliography: No
Index: Yes
Level: Intermediate–Advanced New Readers

Science and Engineering

Adkins, Jan E. ***Toolchest: A Primer of Woodcraft.*** New York: Walker, 1973.

Pages: 48
Series: —

Anyone who enjoys working with wood, who is interested in doing so, or needs to identify the materials necessary to accomplish a specific task will find this primer of hand-worked woodcraft totally satisfying. The text begins with a word about respect and understanding of the wood, which originates from a precious living tree. The anatomy of a tree is followed by an explanation of grains and the distinct qualities of a variety of woods. A chart of strengths, stability, hardness, workability, finish, and uses by wood type is extremely well done.

The author then opens up a carpenter's treasured chest of classic hand tools and clearly explains and illustrates the appearance and use of each tool, whether for measuring, cutting, shaping, boring, doweling, fastening, or sharpening. Different varieties of nails and screws are clearly identified. Although this is an excellent primer for adults at any reading level, beginners may have difficulty with the explanatory text. The illustrations and accompanying labels speak for themselves.

Glossary: No
Bibliography: No
Index: Yes
Level: Intermediate–Advanced New Readers

Asimov, Isaac. *Science Fiction: Vision of Tomorrow?* Revised and updated by Richard Hantula. Milwaukee, WI: Gareth Stevens, 2005.

Pages: 32
Series: Isaac Asimov's 21st Century Library of the Universe

The instruments and spacecraft necessary to explore the universe and gather data on its origins, black holes, colliding galaxies, quasars, and more are a reality. Amazingly, prior to scientific discoveries, science fiction authors were remarkably prescient in their imaginings and inventions. This book presents an intriguing comparison of science fiction with science fact.

Short, well-illustrated chapters look at early science fiction and such writers as Jules Verne and H.G. Wells. *Star Trek* is notable because the space travelers did not experience zero gravity. Science fiction writers invented other worlds, some imagining that planets were pretty much like Earth—with an atmosphere, flora and fauna, and intelligent life forms. Air flight and space travel were made possible with small planes, dirigibles, rocket belts, and rocket ships. Predictions of the future by science fiction writers were truly fantastic, but many ficticious inventions are reality today. A chart, "Modern Inventions That Were Once the Dreams of Science Fiction Writers" follows the text and lists inventions, writers who predicted them, in which work (with date of publication), along with the date of the actual invention. This is a fascinating title, bound to intrigue adult science fiction buffs looking for research linking science fiction with science fact.

Glossary: Yes
Bibliography: Yes, of books, DVDs, and Web sites about science
     fiction and space exploration, and museums and centers with
     sci-fi or space exploration exhibits
Index: Yes
Level: Beginning–Advanced New Readers

Berger, Melvin. *Scholastic Science Dictionary.* Illustrated by Hannah Bonner. New York: Scholastic, 2000.

Pages: 224
Series: —

The stated purpose of this book is to provide a quick and easy way for "young people to familiarize themselves with the vocabulary, ideas, objects and people of science." The term "young people" can be easily ignored by adults looking for a basic dictionary. The book contains over 2,400 entries on topics from the major branches of science. There are also entries for many diseases, drugs, treatments, and specialties in the field of medicine, as well as over 140 short biographies of significant scientists in a variety of fields. The labeled and captioned illustrations add clarity to the definitions. Phonetic pronunciation appears in parentheses after each entry. From Aa to Zygote, each entry is clearly defined. An index of picture labels is included. This title is a solid basic reference source.

Glossary: No
Bibliography: No, but includes a list of resources—museums, magazines, science competitions, and Web sites
Index: No
Level: Intermediate–Advanced New Readers

Boekhoff, P.M. and Stuart A. Kallen. *Lasers.* San Diego, CA: Kidhaven Press, 2002.

Pages: 48
Series: Kidhaven Science Library

A brief definition of the laser is followed by a history of its development from Alexander Graham Bell's concept, to Albert Einstein's theory of stimulated emission of light resulting in greater light amplification, to the basic principles of laser technology used by the six scientists credited with creating the first laser beam. The authors survey the use of lasers in the military, in scientific research (to create accurate maps, understand earthquakes, monitor air pollution, for example), in medicine (surgery), and in industry and recreation. The book ends with a look at the future of laser technology. Color photos enhance the pages, along with a few diagrams. If the word "Kid" in the series title and publisher's name, along with the fairly large print, can be ignored, adults will also find the book useful as a quick reference to laser technology.

Glossary: Yes
Bibliography: Yes, annotated
Index: Yes
Level: Beginning New Readers

Bridgman, Roger. *1000 Inventions and Discoveries.* New York: DK, 2002.

Pages: 256
Series: —

Beginning with stone tools (circa 3,000,000 BC) and ending with self-cleaning glass, invented by British chemist Kevin Sanderson, Bridgman presents a comprehensive survey of life-changing inventions and discoveries. The book is arranged chronologically, with each chapter covering a distinct historical period. The pages are packed with color illustrations that complement the brief text. Some entries are in larger boxes, with somewhat longer explanations, while expanded entries (i.e., for the telephone, radium, theory of relativity, and antibiotics) cover two full pages. There is a running time line along the bottom of each page that notes historical and scientific events that happened at the same time as the inventions and discoveries presented. A brief introduction explains the arrangement of the book and the content of each entry. There are some references to related entries on other pages. Produced in association with the Smithsonian Institution, this title is an attractive source for ready-reference and enjoyable for browsing.

Glossary: No
Bibliography: No
Index: Yes, of inventions and discoveries and of inventors and
    discoverers
Level: Advanced New Readers

Burnett, Betty. *The Laws of Motion: Understanding Uniform and Accelerated Motion.* New York: Rosen, 2005.

Pages: 48
Series: The Library of Physics

The book begins with a definition of the laws of motion, a major part of the science of physics. The author then presents the concept of classical or Newtonian physics, which addresses how matter responds to forces and how forces act on matter. Indeed, most basic laws in physics are about motion. Chapters One and Two describe motion and related concepts—vectors, speed, velocity, uniform motion, acceleration, distance, and displacement. Mechanics, the branch of physics concerned with motion and its two parts, kinematics (how objects move) and dynamics (forces and energy to explain why objects move in a particular way), are described. Various kinds of motion (linear, circular, rotary, projectile) are explained. Chapters Three and Four cover Newton's laws of motion and the forces that act on motion. Excellent photos and diagrams clarify the text. Highlighted boxes present information on the increasing land speed record (miles per hour), kinematics, use of cue balls to demonstrate the law of conservation, and momentum and G forces.

The last chapter, "Describing Motion with Graphs," discusses the language of motion, which is mainly mathematical, using simple diagrams. Any adult studying this aspect of physics for the first time will find this title a useful resource. It also serves as a reference tool for those looking for a quick reference guide to the subject.

Glossary: Yes
Bibliography: Yes, preceded by a list of organizations, Web sites, and books for further reading
Index: Yes
Level: Beginning–Advanced New Readers

Caron, Lucille and Philip M. St. Jacques. *Fractions and Decimals.* Berkeley Heights, NJ: Enslow, 2000.

Pages: 64
Series: Math Success

Understanding fractions and decimals is important to many aspects of life, from calculating the prices of items in dollars and cents or pounds and ounces, to reducing or increasing recipes to suit the number of people served, to interpreting surveys of all sorts and finding ratios. In 28 double-page chapters, the authors explain and illustrate identifying proper, improper, and mixed numbers; comparing equivalent fractions; ordering fractions; renaming fractions as decimals; adding and subtracting like and unlike fractions; multiplying and dividing fractions and mixed numbers; estimating fractions and percentages; reading and writing decimals and percentages; working with decimals as fractions; and understanding repeating decimals. This book is a handy source for quick review of functions not frequently used and appropriate for mathematically challenged adults.

Glossary: No
Bibliography: Yes, of books and Web sites
Index: Yes
Level: Intermediate–Advanced New Readers

Foltz-Jones, Charlotte. *Mistakes That Worked: 40 Familiar Inventions and How They Came to Be.* Illustrated by John O'Brien. Collingdale, PA: DIANE Publishing, 1998.

Pages: 81
Series: —

A delightful collection of stories, this book presents great inventions that came about by accident. Some of the data are historical, while other entries are based on either legend or tales of questionable accuracy, as the truth about the origins of some inventions is lost in history. The selections include an interesting assortment of mistakes and accidents involving foods (Brown and Serve rolls, cheese, chocolate chip cookies, Coca-Cola, doughnut holes, fudge, ice cream cones, maple syrup, popsicles, potato chips, sandwiches, tea, and tea bags);

medical improvements (aspirin, seeing-eye dogs, penicillin, X-rays); recreational items (Frisbees, piggy banks, Silly Putty, Slinkies); places (Jellico, Tennessee; Bangor, Maine; the Leaning Tower of Pisa; Nome, Alaska; and South Dakota's western boundary); clothing (Velcro, leotards, Levi's jeans, trouser cuffs); and, finally, a potpourri of things such as bricks, glass, glassblowing and safety glass, Ivory soap, paper towels, Post-it notes, vulcanized rubber, and Scotch-guard. Additional information and odd facts end many of the presentations. That the text is enriched by humorous color illustrations reminiscent of *The New Yorker* is no surprise, because John O'Brien created many of the magazine's covers. The last page has a brief description of the National Inventors Hall of Fame. Evidence that this is a children's title (found in a first page reference cautioning children wishing to try out the Toll House cookie and fudge recipes to ask for permission from a parent or other adult) should not affect the choice of this well-researched book for adult readers.

Glossary: No
Bibliography: Yes, of secondary sources limited to adult books
Index: Yes
Level: Intermediate New Readers

Fridell, Ron. *Genetic Engineering.* Minneapolis: Lerner, 2006.

Pages: 48
Series: Cool Science

Genetic engineers work to increase crop harvests, heal the sick, and clean up the environment. "Genetics" is defined as the study of the genome, "nature's instructions for growing a specific plant or animal and keeping it alive." Fridell's clear definition of terms is followed by a brief history of genetic engineering in plants, animals, and humans (gene therapy, stem cell repair) that includes a look at the controversy surrounding its use, especially with regard to humans— asking whether it is good science or going against nature. The author presents both positive and negative arguments (improved, larger fruits or vegetables vs. possible allergy; improving animal size to yield more meat; selective breeding; designer children; and more). The book ends with two thought-provoking questions for readers of all ages, urging them on to more in-depth thinking and research: "So why shouldn't parents be allowed to shape their children's genomes too? What do you think?"

The text is clarified by full-color photographs and three charts illustrating, respectively, the human cell and the locations of chromasomes, genes, and DNA; how a supersized mouse was invented; and how Dolly, the sheep, was cloned. Fact pages, highlighted in yellow, contain additional pertinent information. Captions are highlighted in yellow ovals outlined in purple. This is a well-researched and objective presentation of a complicated topic. It serves as an introduction to the subject and a starting point for those interested in further research.

Glossary: Yes
Bibliography: Yes, of books and Web sites
Index: Yes
Level: Intermediate–Advanced New Readers

Johnson, Rebecca L. *Nanotechnology.* Minneapolis: Lerner, 2006.

Pages: 48
Series: Cool Science

In her introduction, Johnson states that nanotechnology made such things as clear sunscreen, stainless clothing, and indestructible car bumpers a reality—and the future promises much more. She clearly and concisely defines nanotechnology as a new science of moving atoms and molecules around to create new things from the bottom up—atom by atom and molecule by molecule. In five chapters, the authors review nanotechnology, new tools to be derived from this new technology (with mention of particular scientists), learning to use nanomaterials (with specific examples), the nanofuture, and nanobots (nanoscale robots). Each page is filled with text and busy with color photos, overlayed with highlighted captions, bright yellow boxes of information on scientists and related nanodata, and fun facts (printed in yellow and green on the pages). This book is a fascinating introduction to the topic.

Glossary: Yes
Bibliography: Yes, of books, periodicals, Web sites; also includes a
    list of books and Web sites for further reading
Index: Yes
Level: Intermediate–Advanced New Readers

Jones, David. *Mighty Robots: Mechanical Marvels That Fascinate and Frighten.* Buffalo, NY: Firefly/Annick, 2005.

Pages: 126
Series: —

Jones's broad survey of robots in film and books is combined with an examination of the development of robotic technology. He discusses the word "robot" and examines the purpose and evolution of robots, the earliest having been built in the 1600s in Japan. Following the first simply designed puppets were those developed by Jacques de Vaucanson in the 1700s. The robotic evolution is traced to the use of artificial intelligence and the mobility achieved thus far and on to the possible future of this complex science. The author focuses on a number of topics, such as Nikola Tesla and telerobotics; Asimov's laws of robotics; solid-state electronics and small computers; Rodney Brooks and artificial intelligence; robots and space exploration; tele-robots; and the use of robots currently in the military, medicine, the home, and play and possibly in the future. The text is enriched by detailed sidebars and numerous clear color photographs with informative captions. This intriguing look at robots in fact and fiction should appeal to adult readers as a short overview as well as a first guide to further resources.

Glossary: No
Bibliography: No
Index: Yes
Level: Intermediate–Advanced New Readers

Lampton, Christopher. *Chemical Accident.* Brookfield, CT: Millbrook, 1994.

Pages: 47
Series: A Disaster! Book

This informative overview of the chemical industry begins with a vivid description of a possible frightening chemical disaster. Then the author quickly assures the reader that such an accident is unlikely to occur and why. Succinct definitions of chemicals, atoms, and molecules are followed by discussions of the importance of chemicals, how chemicals react, how the chemical industry uses them to make a variety of things (soap, dyes, rubber, fertilizer), and what can be done to prevent chemical accidents and injury or death when an accident does occur. A chapter on the disaster in Bhopal, India, is followed by one that lists other chemical disasters. The illustrations serve to clarify the text.

Glossary: Yes
Bibliography: Yes
Index: Yes
Level: Beginning New Readers

Macaulay, David. *The New Way Things Work.* Boston: Houghton Mifflin, 1998.

Pages: 400
Series: —

An expanded, updated version of the 1988 title, this book looks at the amazing workings of machines, from the simplest device to the complicated workings of the Internet. Macaulay effectively demonstrates how a concept behind one invention is indeed linked to a concept behind another. This comprehensive work is divided into five parts: "The Mechanics of Movement," "Harnessing the Elements," "Working With Waves," "Electricity & Automation," and "The Digital Domain." The workings of the grand piano, electric mixer, airship, toilet tank, rocket engine, record player, quartz clock, automatic door, airbag, computer mouse, magnetic storage, and a robot, to name just a few devices, are explained with brief text, humorous drawings, and diagrams with detailed captions and labels. The book closes with the section "Eureka!: The Invention of Machines," a list of and brief data on various inventions, including the zipper, parking meter, bicycle, and space probe. The final section is a list of technical terms. A captivating visual delight, this book is jam-packed with information that is easy to understood. It is both a ready-reference title and a book for browsing.

Glossary: No
Bibliography: No
Index: Yes
Level: Intermediate–Advanced New Readers

Orr, Tamra. *The Telescope.* New York: Franklin Watts, 2004.

Pages: 80
Series: Inventions That Shaped the World

Orr begins with a look at ancient conceptions of the universe, including Aristotle's idea of a geocentric system (with Earth at the center), the theory of a perfect planet, Copernicus' heliocentric philosophy (with the sun as center), early map making (the Flemish cartographer Gerardus Mercator; 1512–1594) and Hans Lippershey's (1570–1619) idea of creating an instrument that led to the development of the modern telescope. One chapter is dedicated to Galileo's research, construction of a telescope, and observations of the universe, which lead him to agree with the Copernican system and thus encounter trouble with the Catholic Church, including a charge of heresy and house arrest. Subsequent chapters trace the perfection of the telescope after Galileo, along with the scientists involved: Isaac Newton, George Elliot Hale (design changes in 1917), Hubble (in 1929), Lyman Spitzer's concept of developing a large telescopic observatory in space, and on to present-day powerful telescopes and NASA's great observatories.

Full-color photo reproductions, color and black-and-white illustrations, and additional boxed information enhance the text. A time line is included, A good primary reference source, this attractive, fact-filled book should appeal to adult readers in need of a comprehensive overview of the subject as well as to the casual reader.

Glossary: Yes
Bibliography: Yes, of books, Web sites, and organizations
Index: Yes
Level: Intermediate New Readers

Oxlade, Chris, Corrine Stockley, and Jane Wertheim. *Illustrated Dictionary of Chemistry.* Tulsa, OK: EDC, 2004.

Pages: 128
Series: Illustrated Dictionaries

This is a handy, comprehensive quick reference to chemistry divided into five main color-coded subject sections: physical chemistry; inorganic chemistry; organic chemistry; environmental chemistry; and general information that includes the metal reactivity series, the properties of the elements, naming simple organic compounds, the laboratory preparation of six gases, laboratory tests, the investigation of chemical substances, qualitative and quantitative analysis, chemical apparatus, units, and data on famous chemists. The definitions and technical terminology are explained in clear language and supported by many captioned illustrations and tables and charts. Main entries appear in bold type throughout the text and in the index. Instructions on how to use the book are easy to follow.

Glossary: Yes
Bibliography: No
Index: Yes, of substances, symbols, formulas, and terms
Level: Advanced New Readers

Oxlade, Chris, Corrine Stockley, and Jane Wertheim. *Illustrated Dictionary of Physics.* Tulsa, OK: EDC, 2004.

Pages: 128
Series: Illustrated Dictionaries

Much more than the usual dictionary, this book provides the reader with a comprehensive illustrated guide to physics. There are six color-coded subject sections: mechanics and general physics; heat energy; wave energy; electricity and magnetism; atomic and nuclear physics; and general data such as quantities and units, equations, symbols and graphs, measurements, accuracy and errors, fields and forces, vectors and scalars, circuit symbols, transistors and gates, elements, and properties of substances. A key to using the book is clearly presented. This is an excellent, comprehensive reference source for all ages.

Glossary: Yes
Bibliography: No
Index: Yes, with main word definitions in boldface
Level: Advanced New Readers

Peacock, Graham. *Electricity.* Chicago: Raintree/Heinemann, 1994.

Pages: 32
Series: Science Activities

Excellent color photographs and diagrams, large type, and simple text make this title a fine source of information on electricity and how it is generated and processed to create the power needed for the many tasks that require it. Explanations of how lightbulbs, thermostats, timepieces, and other electricity-dependent devices work will satisfy the adult beginning reader. Simple projects for children, such as lighting a lightbulb, making a switch, and setting up a circuit with a conductor and an insulator, could be of interest to an adult new to the subject. Knowledge of how electricity works is useful to everyone.

Glossary: Yes, of key terms that appear in boldface within the text
Bibliography: Yes
Index: Yes
Level: Beginning New Readers

Sandler, Martin W. *Inventors.* New York: HarperCollins, 1999.

Pages: 96
Series: Library of Congress Classics

The reader is allowed to step back into the nineteenth century, when America's spirit of adventure and inventiveness flourished, and then to follow the history of phenomenal creativity into the twentieth century. Facts about famous inventors and the impact they had on American life are blended with descriptions of the products of invention: the telegraph, sewing machine, typewriter, motion picture projector, electric lightbulb, telephone, steel, airplane, steam engine, bicycle, trolley, railway systems, automobile, photography, and more. The easy-to-read text flows along with the many reproductions of photographs, paintings, posters, lithographs, and other illustrations from the Library of Congress archives and one photograph from NASA. Meaningful quotations (with source and date) in highlighted boxes enhance the presentation. The final page reveals a bit of information on the mission, collections, and history of the Library of Congress.

In his brief introduction, James Billington, the Librarian of Congress, states that the goal of this series of children's books is to enrich "our greatest natural resource—the minds and imaginations of our young people." This aim most certainly applies to adult readers as well.

Glossary: No
Bibliography: No
Index: Yes, with page references to the photographs in italic
Level: Intermediate–Advanced New Readers

Sayre, April Pulley. *Secrets of Sound: Studying the Calls and Songs of Whales, Elephants, and Birds.* New York: Houghton Mifflin, 2002.

Pages: 64
Series: Scientists in the Field

Sayre defines bioacoustics—the scientific study of animal sounds—and discusses our relatively new ability to explore the sounds that animals make that are beyond the normal range of human hearing. The purpose of this branch of science is to understand what the sounds mean and apply this knowledge to save endangered species. Three bioacousticians are introduced: Christopher Clark (who studies whales), Katy Payne (who studies elephants in the wild and in zoos), and Bill Evans (who studies night-migrating birds). This close-up look at three researchers at work in the field includes some biographical information about how their early interests led them to bioacoustics. A fascinating, fact-filled text, the book has ample clear color photos and is further enhanced by direct quotes. A thoughtful look at the future of bioacoustics completes this fascinating glimpse of a little-known field of study.

Glossary: Yes
Bibliography: Yes, of books, animal sound recordings, articles, and
     research organizations
Index: Yes
Level: Intermediate–Advanced New Readers

Silverstein, Alvin, Virginia Silverstein, and Laura Silverstein Nunn. *DNA.* Brookfield, CT: Twenty-First Century Books, 2002.

Pages: 64
Series: Science Concepts

Adults looking for a compact but detailed explanation of DNA, RNA, cell structure, the role of amino acids and heredity, DNA mutations, the Genome Project, use of DNA for solving crimes and revealing clues to the past, and genetic engineering will find this book useful. Controversial issues concerning tinkering, cloning, and gene therapy are discussed from different viewpoints and in an unbiased manner. There are clear color photo reproductions, diagrams, and ample sidebars to enhance the text. This is a fine introduction to a complex subject.

Glossary: Yes
Bibliography: Yes, of books, videos, and Internet resources
Index: Yes
Level: Intermediate–Advanced New Readers

Slavin, Bill. *Transformed: How Everyday Things Are Made.*
Tonawanda, NY: Kids Can Press, 2005.

Pages: 160
Series: —

Chickle is processed to remove bark, bugs, and other impurities before it becomes chewing gum. In 1948, a Michigan housewife's cat's sandbox sand froze, so she borrowed a few cups of dried clay pellets for her cat box—giving birth to kitty litter. The first toothpaste was moistened ground marble, so a kid using it would have rocks in his head while brushing his teeth. These are just a few of the 69 commonplace things that Slavin, in double-page spreads, delightfully recounts the evolution of. The book is divided into five sections: "Fun and Games" includes such things as baseballs, CDs, chewing gum, ship-in-a-bottle, and teddy bears; "Around the House" solves the mystery of how things like cat litter, dental floss, matches, and plastic wrap evolved; "Soup to Nuts" looks at food—bread, chocolate, fortune cookies, jelly beans, licorice, tea and yogurt; "Cover-Ups" includes items like blue jeans, polyester, running shoes, silk and work gloves; and the final chapter, "Back to Basics," looks at the raw materials used to make many of the items listed—aluminum, brick, cement, glass, paper, lumber, plastic resins, petroleum, and rubber.

The information is presented in easy-to-follow numbered steps. The descriptions are clear, but there is an abundance of undefined terminology. This would be a flaw, but Slavin's very appealing cartoon drawings, complete with engaging elfin workers, take over to clarify what is not defined in the text. A brief introduction to each process provides a short history of each item. The book answers questions children ask and satisfies adult curiosity about the origins of everyday things they might wonder about. This is a bright and breezy reference source.

Glossary: Yes
Bibliography: Yes, of books, encyclopedias, and videos
Index: Yes
Level: Beginning–Advanced New Readers

Viegas, Jennifer. *Kinetic and Potential Energy: Understanding Changes Within Physical Systems.* New York: Rosen, 2005.

Pages: 48
Series: The Library of Physics

A definition of physics as the study of matter, energy, and motion begins the book. There are also explications of the sun as our energy supply, the process of photosynthesis, and the role of fossil fuels as sources of energy. The definitions of potential energy and kinetic energy are notable for their clarity—progressing from an explanation of potential energy to elastic potential energy, chemical potential energy, gravitational potential energy, joules (a metric system unit of measurement used to measure work or energy), and kinetic energy. Formulas to calculate gravitational potential energy, joules, and kinetic energy are clearly explained.

Subsequent chapters explain mechanical energy—work (a force that acts upon an object to cause a displacement), friction and air resistance, how roller coasters work, the work–energy theorem (including how it applies to a moving bike), the law of inertia, momentum, conservation of momentum, how energy and momentum laws help athletes, and how airplanes stay in the air. Captioned photo illustrations and a few good diagrams clarify the text. Fact boxes explain calories, why car tires have treads, why humans generate a lot of heat, and turning one's hand into an airplane by creating air pressure change. This title serves as a quick reference source and review guide for adults.

Glossary: Yes
Bibliography: Yes, preceded by a further reading section including
    magazines, Web sites, and books
Index: Yes
Level: Intermediate–Advanced New Readers

Walker, Richard. *Genes & DNA*. Boston: Kingfisher, 2007.

Pages: 64
Series: Kingfisher Knowledge

In just three chapters, Walker provides readers with an exploration of genes and DNA. Chapter 1 looks at genes and the code of life—a set of instructions that determines inheritance. Walker mentions Gregor Mendel, whose work became the basis of the science of genetics, an explication of cells and chromosomes, gene variation, sex chromosomes, environment as a behavior determinant, and how multiple births occur. Chapter 2, titled "DNA: The Molecule of Life," explains the discovery of the structure of DNA—the material from which genes are made—how DNA works, changes in the instructions that control cells and mutations, the Human Genome Project, genes, and evolution. Chapter 3 covers genetic technology, including DNA fingerprinting, tracing ancestors, genetic engineering, screening for diseases, gene therapy, cloning, transplantation, stem cell research, DNA and extinct and endangered species, identifying specific genes in geonomes, and future research and discoveries.

Each chapter ends with a half-page summary, as well as definitions of the roles of various types of scientists, for example, geneticist, microbiologist, and genetic counselor, and sources for further information (museums, zoos, etc.), giving names of institutions, addresses, telephone numbers, and Web sites.

Exceptional captioned photographs and illustrations illuminate the fascinating facts and explanations provided in the text. An impressive, well-written introduction to the subject, the book serves as a primary source and summary of the topic for adult readers.

Glossary: Yes
Bibliography: Yes, of organizations, including Web sites, at the end of each chapter
Index: Yes
Level: Beginning–Intermediate New Readers

Wallace, Joseph. *The Lightbulb.* New York: Atheneum Books for Young Readers, 1999.

Pages: 80
Series: Turning Point Inventions

A history of the search for a safe, clean light source—from firelight to candles, whale oil lamps, kerosene lamps to natural gas, and more, Wallace traces the development of the lightbulb and Edison's work to perfect it. The book concludes with a look at the future of the technology.

With the exception of a few references to the intended youthful audience, an adult who can bypass this will find the book an interesting read. Full-color and black-and-white photo reproductions illuminate the text. Captions add further information, but, unfortunately, their print is small and light in color, making them difficult to read. A foldout page of illustrations summarizing the development of the lightbulb is remarkable. This title is a handy, nutshell history for the adult reader.

Glossary: No
Bibliography: Yes
Index: Yes
Level: Beginning–Advanced New Readers

Wilkinson, Philip and Jacqueline Dineen. *Art and Technology Through the Ages.* New York: Chelsea House, 1994.

Pages: 96
Series: Ideas That Changed the World

Art and technology are usually not linked, but this book tells the story of how art inspired inventions and how technological developments influenced the creation of various forms of art. For example, the discovery of new materials (from cave walls to paper) and the invention of the printing press made books and information widely accessible; the potter's wheel, better kilns, and improved glassmaking techniques resulted in the creation of beautiful pottery, fine porcelain, and glass designs; the discovery of various metals and the invention of stronger and improved tools led to the creation of a variety of architectural designs and the fine art of jewelry making; and the evolution of verbal communication, from smoke signals to radio, television, sound recordings, tape cassettes, compact discs, and motion picture technology is linked to the history of music and the performing arts. Each brief chapter traces the development of inventions (the steel-making process, printing press, microscope, voice transmission, computer, etc.) that had a profound effect on the quality of life. The color illustrations and highlighted boxes containing additional information support the text.

Glossary: No
Bibliography: Yes
Index: Yes
Level: Intermediate–Advanced New Readers

Woodford, Chris and Martin Clowes. *Atoms and Molecules.*
Farmington Hills, MI: Thomson Gale, 2004.

Pages: 40
Series: Routes of Science

The authors provide a surprisingly in-depth examination of the subject in these relatively few pages. Quantum theory and ancient philosophers and alchemists and their theories of matter are introduced before the first chapter. The authors summarize the origins of alchemy before discussing early chemists, the emergence of theories and processes used to break down and identify component elements, and discovering how component elements are related to one another. Additional chapters look at the scientists involved with molecules, matter and motion, and atoms; the discovery of radioactivity and different types of radiation; and the theory of the nuclear atom. A final chapter looks at the future and the roles of the quantum theory, particle accelerations, quarks, and nanotechnology.

The explanations of how theories developed over time are clear and concise. Important names and terms appear in boldface and are also circled to guide the reader to additional information in boxed areas and sidebars. There are brief biographies of scientists, theorists, and inventors and mention of significant experiments and the conclusions drawn from them. This title is rich with color photographs, illustrations, and diagrams that help explain concepts and discoveries. It is a fascinating look at the subject and a good ready-reference source for adult readers.

Glossary: Yes
Bibliography: Yes, of books and Web sites
Index: Yes
Level: Beginning–Advanced New Readers

Social Sciences

Dash, Joan. *We Shall Not Be Moved: The Women's Factory Strike of 1909.* New York: Scholastic, 1998.

Pages: 165
Series: —

This is an exciting, realistic account of the working conditions in the shirtwaist factories in the Lower East Side of New York City. The working conditions were appalling for the young women workers, who were mostly Jewish (from Russia and Poland) and Italian immigrants. The harsh life of these poor, underpaid, unskilled, undernourished women eventually created an atmosphere of active rebellion, which resulted in the 1909 strike. Clara Lemlich, a shirtwaist girl, was responsible for the formation of Local 25 of the ILGWU (International Ladies Garment Workers Union). This weak union caused other alliances to be formed, most significantly, the Women's Trade Union League, with a membership of middle-aged, educated, and rich society women who had the means and influence to speak out actively for reform. One famous woman was Mrs. Alva Belmont, a great crusader for women's rights. The author points out that the most important result of the strike was the union of women of all classes in support of reform. A few photographs and other illustrations are quite dramatic.

Glossary: No
Bibliography: Yes
Index: Yes
Level: Advanced New Readers

Frisch, Carlienne. *Hearing the Pitch: Evaluating All Kinds of Advertising.* New York: Rosen, 1994.

Pages: 48
Series: Life Skills

This practical guide to the advertising industry provides a succinct lesson in the techniques used to influence consumers. It tells how to analyze the message and how to ask questions about advertisements in order to make informed choices. The author defines types of advertising (institutional, product, and public service), traces the history and purpose of advertising, and discusses how to hear and appropriately utilize the pitch of all those media ads—from television, radio, magazines, newspapers, direct mail, billboards, and more. By following a case study, the reader learns how to avoid false advertisements by examining the language of the ad carefully and checking with the Better Business Bureau. Black-and-white and color photographs complement the text. Although the book is clearly aimed at a juvenile audience, it can provide adults with quick answers to questions on how to compare information in order to benefit from advertising.

Glossary: No
Bibliography: Yes
Index: Yes
Level: Intermediate New Readers

Good, Diane L. *Brown v. Board of Education.* New York: Children's Press, 2004.

Pages: 48
Series: Cornerstones of Freedom, Second Series

Numerous captioned photos illuminate the differences that existed between white and segregated schools and the steps taken toward integration. This modest text traces the history of segregation in the United States and the cases that tested the law and put energy into the movement toward integration. The Supreme Court decision in *Brown v. Board of Education,* handed down on May 17, 1954, ruled for desegregation—a decision that marked the beginning of a long fight for equality and equal rights for African Americans. This title provides a handy ready-reference source for basic facts.

Glossary: Yes
Bibliography: Yes, of books and Web sites
Index: Yes
Level: Beginning–Intermediate New Readers

Jacobs, William J. *Ellis Island: New Hope in a New Land.* Louisville, KY: American Printing House for the Blind, 1993.

Pages: 34
Series: —

A 1670 survey map of Manhattan and black-and-white photographs of new immigrants viewing the Manhattan skyline for the first time, people packed in a ship's steerage area, people crowded into the halls of Ellis Island undergoing health tests and waiting to enter the country after approval, immigrant faces, Ellis Island in ruins and in the process of restoration, people viewing the Statue of Liberty and the Immigrant Wall of Honor, and more fill this picture book. Together with its well-written, poignant text, it is a remarkable source of facts on the role Ellis Island played in the history of immigration as well as on its present importance as a museum created in honor of those who sought a new life in this country. The type is large and easy to read, while the text brings the human experience of Ellis Island to life.

Glossary: No
Bibliography: No
Index: Yes
Level: Beginning New Readers

Johnston, Norma. *Remember the Ladies: The First Women's Rights Convention.* New York: Scholastic, 1995.

Pages: 176
Series: —

The author recounts the history of events that culminated in the first women's rights convention held at Seneca Falls, New York, in 1848. The book includes the story of Elizabeth Cady Stanton's life and descriptions of other important figures, including Lucretia Mott and Frederick Douglass. There is a chronology of the women's rights movement to 1920, a list of sources of quotations appearing throughout the text, and numerous photographs and fascimilies of significant documents. Well written, this memorable title is an excellent source for adults seeking data on this particular period or on women's rights in general.

Glossary: No
Bibliography: Yes
Index: Yes, with page references to the illustrations in italic
Level: Advanced New Readers

Jones, Rebecca C. *The President Has Been Shot! True Stories of the Attacks on Ten U.S. Presidents.* Madison, WI: Turtleback Books, 1998.

Pages: 134
Series: —

This detailed account of four American presidents who were assassinated—Abraham Lincoln, James A. Garfield, William McKinley, and John Fitzgerald Kennedy—and the six who survived the attempts on their lives—Andrew Jackson, Theodore Roosevelt, Franklin D. Roosevelt, Harry S. Truman, Gerald Ford, and Ronald Reagan— goes beyond the usual history book presentation. It examines the lives, warped minds, motives, plots, arrests, and fates of the assailants. Anecdotes, obscure bits of information, and poignant quotations bring the horror of the attacks to life. Historic black-and-white drawings and photographs enhance this highly readable, well-researched look at the dark side of the presidency.

Glossary: No
Bibliography: Yes, a two-page textual account of where to locate more information in newspapers, magazines, and books and at the assassination sites

Index: Yes, with page references to illustrations in italic
Level: Beginning—Intermediate New Readers

Landau, Elaine. *The Abolitionist Movement.* New York:
Children's Press, 2004.

Pages: 48
Series: Cornerstones of Freedom, Second Series

This discussion of the abolitionist movement begins with a glimpse
at the pre–Civil War period, when slavery was legal and millions of
Africans were brought to this country on slave ships. The movement is
traced, including the events and the people involved in working for
change, from increasing momentum to abolish slavery in the northern
states to the end of the Civil War in April 1865 and the ratification of
the Thirteenth Amendment in December of the same year. Women's
involvement in the abolitionist movement is discussed, as are the
people who were prominent in the fight against slavery, such as,
David Walker, William Lloyd Garrison, Nat Turner, Frederick Douglass,
Lucretia Mott, Harriet Tubman, Sojourner Truth, and, of course,
Abraham Lincoln. This brief examination of the slavery era provides
the reader with a compact history, amply illustrated with photo illustrations and a few reproductions of pertinent documents. A time
line is included. This title is a quick reference source for a complex
and detailed subject.

Glossary: Yes
Bibliography: Yes
Index: Yes
Level: Beginning–Intermediate New Readers

Landau, Elaine. *Women's Right to Vote.* New York: Children's
Press, 2005.

Pages: 48
Series: Cornerstones of Freedom, Second Series

The author begins her discussion of the fight to gain women the
right to vote with the first public conference on women's rights in

1848 at Seneca Falls, New York. She clearly highlights the suffrage movement up to 1920, when the Nineteenth Amendment was signed into law. Brief biographical data on outstanding leaders and activists, such as Elizabeth Cady Stanton, Lucy Stone, Susan B. Anthony, Anna Howard Shaw, Carrie Chapman Catt, and Alice Paul are included. This clearly written book, with ample photo illustrations and a time line, is a useful quick reference source.

Glossary: Yes
Bibliography: Yes, of books and Web sites
Index: Yes
Level: Beginning–Intermediate New Readers

McWhorter, Diane. *A Dream of Freedom: The Civil Rights Movement from 1954 to 1968.* New York: Scholastic, 2004.

Pages: 154
Series: —

A foreword by Reverend Fred Shuttlesworth introduces this history of the movement to make the Constitution's declaration that "all men are created equal" a reality. The author, a white girl growing up in Birmingham, provides a frank account of her own racist upbringing and an excellent chronological history of the struggle for freedom and the end to segregation. McWhorter examines the beginning of segregation, defining the "segregated mind." She then devotes chapters to *Brown v. Board of Education*, the Montgomery bus boycott, Little Rock, the sit-ins, the freedom rides, Birmingham, the march on Washington, Selma, Watts, Chicago, Malcolm X, the Black Panthers, Memphis, and more in sections defined by dates from 1954 to 1968. The text is enhanced by photo reproductions containing powerful images. There are highlighted text boxes with informative captions on related subjects, such as the lynch law, Scottsboro, Thurgood Marshall, the white south revolts, Fred Shuttlesworth, Medgar Evers, the church bombers, children of Birmingham, and the FBI versus Martin Luther King. An emotion-filled, detailed accounting of the Civil Rights movement, this title is a well-researched, powerfully written reference source.

Glossary: No
Bibliography: Yes, a full-page selected list and a separate list of Web
    sites and books for further reading
Index: Yes
Level: Intermediate–Advanced New Readers

Spies, Karen Bornemann. *Our Money.* Brookfield, CT:
Millbrook, 2001.

Pages: 48
Series: I Know America

This book is perfect for anyone seeking answers to common questions about paper money and coins, such as what is a Federal Reserve Note, what is printed on the two sides of paper money, how do you decipher the coding on bills, what is on each coin, what are coins made of, what do you do with worn-out or mutilated money, and what determines the value of coins in a collection. A brief history provides facts about the money of early civilizations, the first American coins and paper money, colonial American money, and Confederate money. Finally, the author touches on numismatics, the current value of money, and how currency might change in the future.

A number of highlighted boxes throughout the text contain related information, such as the images that appear on the front and back of U.S. bills and coins, the origins of the pictures used on the various denominations, a list of terms used in the making of coins, facts about counterfeiters, attempts made to rob the federal mint, and who to contact for information on collecting money. The numerous illustrations and a chronology add to the book's usefulness. This brief title is filled with a surprising amount of information and is a good ready-reference source.

Glossary: No
Bibliography: Yes
Index: Yes
Level: Beginning–Intermediate New Readers

Stafford, James. *The European Union: Facts and Figures.*
Broomall, PA: Mason Crest, 2006.

Pages: 88
Series: —

This in-depth, up-to-date look at the European Union (EU) opens to a color-coded map of the EU members, followed by an account of the origins of the EU with the creation of the ECSC (European Coal and Steel Community) by the Treaty of Paris in 1951—a common market in coal and steel with the aim of allowing goods to move freely across borders without the paper work and customs duties. In 1958, the ECSC evolved into the European Economic Community, which, because of social and living conditions, the eventually evolved into the EU that is presently in place. It is the world's second largest economy with a single currency shared by 12 member countries.

Concise explanations of how the EU works, the EU and the European economy, the EU and a knowledge-based society (educational, government services, health and entertainment services with origins in technological improvements), the function of the EU, its role in securing freedom, security and justice, and the EU and the future—difficulties and challenges—are well presented.

The book is rich with quick fact boxes (subjects include the past and future of the EU, the EU presidents, and the number of votes cast by member states), captioned photo illustrations, cartoon-like pictures, and informative charts and graphs. A chronology is included. There is a page of project and report ideas adult readers can easily ignore. This is a visually satisfying, concise study of the EU that serves adults looking for basic information.

Glossary: Yes, words included appear in boldface within the
   text
Bibliography: Yes, of books, Internet sources, and
   organizations
Index: Yes
Level: Intermediate New Readers

Summer, Lila E. and Samuel G. Woods. *The Judiciary.*
Austin, TX: Steck-Vaughn, 1997.

Pages: 48
Series: Good Citizenship Library

This large-print book addresses the complicated subject of law: why laws are made; what laws mean to the nation, the community, and the individual; and how laws can be challenged and changed to reflect new needs and new philosophies. For example, traffic laws were revised when the automobile took over the roads, and copyright laws had to be updated to include nonprint media such as videotape and computer software. A discussion of landmark cases, such as *Miranda v. Arizona* (guaranteeing the right of the accused to silence and consultation with a lawyer), *Mapp v. Ohio* (stating that evidence against the accused could not be used unless it was obtained legally), *Brown v. Board of Education of Topeka* (public school segregation by state law is unconstitutional), amplifies the text. Captioned photographs and pictures and a simple chart of the state and federal court systems add to the information in the book. This title is an excellent way to introduce U.S. law to beginning adult readers, particularly to those preparing for U.S. citizenship.

Glossary: Yes
Bibliography: Yes, of secondary sources but limited to children's books
Index: Yes
Level: Beginning New Readers

✺ Sports ✺

Anderson, Dave. *The Story of the Olympics.* New York: William Morrow, 2000.

Pages: 168
Series: —

The history of the Olympics is traced from its origins in ancient Greece to the present modern international festivals of the summer and winter games. The first part covers the phenomenon of the Olympics, with highlights of the games, great athletes, political disruptions, the invasion of big business, and the crass commercialism that has taken over the competitions. The second part examines the competitive spirit of individual athletes in the fields of track and field, gymnastics, swimming and diving, figure skating, skiing, and a few other sports and highlights the achievements of such notable athletes as Carl Lewis, Al Oerter, Wilma Rudolph, Nadia Comaneci, Mark Spitz, Katarina Witt, Oksana Baiul, Bonnie Blair, Kristie Yamaguchi, Picabo Street, and Dan Jansen. A final chapter discusses why the Olympics are eternally popular. They never go stale, and, unlike any other sporting event, the games are held in various locations around the world. Numerous black-and-white photographs of the athletes in action add to the appeal of this book.

Glossary: No
Bibliography: No
Index: Yes, with page references to photographs in boldface
Level: Beginning New Readers

Bailey, John. *Fishing.* New York: DK, 2001.

Pages: 48
Series: Superguides

Fishing expert John Bailey addresses a young adult audience in his brief introduction, but the book serves the adult novice fisherman as well. It opens with a single-page history of fishing—a sport for about 3,000 years. The pages are packed with information on the anatomy and life cycle of a fish and the eating habits of various species; necessary fishing gear, including flies, lures, bait, and bobbers; and lessons on casting technique, bottom and surf fishing, how to play and land the fish, releasing the catch, and more. Clear color illustrations, accompanied by detailed captions, successfully demonstrate fishing techniques and bring the reader right to the scene so well that one can almost hear the insects buzz and the water lapping.

Glossary: Yes
Bibliography: No, but has a useful list of addresses
Index: Yes
Level: Beginning–Intermediate New Reader

Buckley, James, Jr. *Football.* New York: DK, 1999.

Pages: 64
Series: Eyewitness

A richly illustrated book with detailed captions and an introductory paragraph for each double-page section, this title looks at the many facets of professional football. It begins with a section on the history of the game, from its origins in the mid-ninteenth century to its evolution from a college to a professional sport with the formation of the NFL (National Football League) in 1920. Other topics include great moments in NFL history, the anatomy of the football, football field specifications, team uniforms, coaches, the design of the helmet and other components of the uniform, game plays and players, strategies used in the game, the training camp, the role of umpires, fans, and more. The book was developed in association with the NFL and is a striking and definitive guide to a most popular sport. A perfect choice for reference or browsing, it will satisfy both fans and those new to the game.

Glossary: No
Bibliography: No
Index: No
Level: Beginning–Intermediate New Reader

Buckley, James, Jr. *Super Bowl.* New York: DK, 2000.

Pages: 64
Series: Eyewitness

Developed in association with the NFL (National Football League), the book opens with a two-page spread that examines football in the years before the Super Bowl and then continues with a look at how it was born—along with the merger of the American Football League with the NFL and Pete Roselle's announcement of the new championship game. Double-page spreads look at the highlights of each Super Bowl game, from I to XXXVI. Sections on trophies, rings, amazing plays, records, coaches, the pre-game and halftime shows, the fans, collectibles, the role of the media, stadiums, and playoff games complete the book. The combination of short explanatory paragraphs, rich color illustrations, and detailed captions provides an excellent source for both reference and browsing.

Glossary: No
Bibliography: No
Index: Yes
Level: Beginning–Intermediate New Readers

Gifford, Clive. *Soccer: The Ultimate Guide to the Beautiful Game.* Revised Edition. Boston: Kingfisher, 2004.

Pages: 96
Series: —

This impressive guide to soccer, the world's most popular sport, combines clear text and marvelous illustrations to present all aspects of the game. An introduction traces the early history of the game and includes a time line (1848–1930) that runs down the right page margin. The book continues with double-page sections covering the field and players, key rules, fouls and misconduct, and the warm-up before the game. A skills section provides excellent practical advice for soccer players on such topics as ball control, tackling, and fancy skills, with remarkable clarity. The next sections cover position and play, set places, the roles of managers and coaches, tactics, pro games (especially in Europe and South America), great competitions, great games, and great players. The book closes with a reference section that includes a two-page history of soccer and a selected list of fascinating statistics. "See Also" page references run along the left page margins. Included are highlighted "Masterclass" boxes giving brief instructions on various aspects of the game and fact boxes with pictures and brief biographical data on notable soccer players. This title is an excellent source for any adult interested in the game, either as a player or a spectator.

Glossary: Yes
Bibliography: No, but has a list of Web sites
Index: Yes
Level: Intermediate–Advanced New Reader

Hammond, Tim and Laura Butler. *Sports.* New York: DK, 2005.

Pages: 72
Series: Eyewitness

This pictorial essay profiles a variety of sports, ranging from soccer, football, basketball, baseball, tennis, and ice hockey to the less widely played cricket, fencing, archery, snooker, and badminton. Each sport is briefly introduced, including a history of the game. Pictures and diagrams illustrate the necessary equipment, the technological advances made to improve the equipment, how uniform styles changed over the years, what the game rules are, and how the various games are played. Visually rich, this informative title is an excellent source of basic sports data.

Glossary: No
Bibliography: No
Index: Yes
Level: Beginning–Intermediate New Reader

Kirkwood, Jon. *Fantastic Book of Car Racing.* Illustrated by Graham White. Brookfield, CT: Copper Beech Books, 1997.

Pages: 32
Series: Fantastic Foldout Book

This is the perfect source for anyone who wants to learn about the history of car racing and understand the design, construction, mechanics, and operation of the different racers. No doubt the reader will be interested to discover how the sport has evolved into one of hi-tech safety methods and rules while retaining the thrill of speed. The contents give concise information on Le Mans racing, drag racing, go-cart racing, rally-car racing, formula one racing, driver's protection, the racing team, racing safety, the world's circuits, types of lap-style car races, endurance races, and racing oddities from trucks to lawnmowers.

Fact boxes contain the specifications for each of the racers. Captioned pictures help explain aerodynamics, boosting the power of the engine, braking and suspension, gears, fuel injection, roll bars, the pits, and more. In addition, there is a foldout section on the Grand Prix that covers qualifying for the race, the race day, the duties of the race officials, and post-race activities. An excellent diagram of the car is included.

Glossary: Yes
Bibliography: No
Index: Yes
Level: Beginning New Readers

Schmidt, Norman. *The Great Kite Book.* Winnepeg, MB: Tamos, 1998.

Pages: 96
Series: —

Let's go fly a kite—a handmade, one-of-a-kind kite! Traditionally, holding onto the string of a kite as it lifts off and is caught by the air currents that send it soaring is more thrilling for many people than watching a world series game or engaging in any other sport. This book provides beginning to experienced kiting enthusiasts with a brief history of kiting and explains the conditions (i.e., wind speed, aerodynamics, stabilizers) necessary for successful kite performance, the materials needed to construct the kites that are discussed in the book, and clear step-by-step instructions, with captioned diagrams for some really exquisite kite designs. The 19 designs should capture the attention of anyone who wants to send one or more unique creations skyward.

Glossary: Yes
Bibliography: Yes
Index: Yes
Level: Intermediate New Readers

Sullivan, George. *All About Football.* New York: Penguin, 1990.

Pages: 128
Series: —

Here is the perfect book for anyone seeking a comprehensive explication of football. The first chapter covers some football fundamentals, such as field dimensions, the difference between high school/college and professional fields, Canadian football compared with the U.S. game, and facts about the ball, scoring, and equipment. Subsequent chapters summarize offense versus defense, rules, penalties, the history of the game, and the careers of some well-known players like Joe Namath, O.J. Simpson, Roger Staubach, Jim Brown, Gale Sayers, and Johnny Unitas. Black-and white photographs, a list of all-time records, and highlighted boxes with additional data (i.e., college football conferences, biggest college football stadiums, American and National Football League conferences, and professional football's longest game) supplement the text.

Glossary: Yes, of football words and terms
Bibliography: No
Index: Yes
Level: Intermediate–Advanced New Readers

Ward, Geoffrey C. and Ken Burns. *Baseball: 25 Great Moments.* New York: Knopf, 1994.

Pages: 61
Series: American Epic

Extracted from the larger volume *Baseball: An Illustrated History,* published in conjunction with the PBS television series *Baseball,* this title captures the drama and excitement of 25 unforgettable baseball moments. Arranged in chronological order beginning in 1846, the year of the first baseball game, and ending in 1993, when Joe Carter hit the home run that won the World Series for the Toronto Blue Jays, the drama of the great moments is effectively captured. Other events recounted involve such baseball greats as Ty Cobb, Babe Ruth, Lou Gehrig, Joe DiMaggio, Jackie Robinson, Willie Mays, Roger Maris, Hank Aaron, and Nolan Ryan. Fast-paced narrative and photographs of baseball greats and historic events result in a lively presentation of memorable chapters in baseball history. This book is an excellent quick reference source.

Glossary: No
Bibliography: No
Index: Yes, with page references to illustrations in boldface
Level: Beginning New Readers

Ward, Geoffrey C., Kenneth Burns, and Paul Robert Walker. *Who Invented the Game? Baseball, the American Epic.* Collingdale, PA: DIANE Publishing, 2004.

Pages: 80
Series: —

In 1905, sporting goods giant Alan Spaulding formed a committee to find out how baseball began. Two years later the committee reported that Abner Doubleday, a schoolboy from Cooperstown, New York, created the rules for a game he called "baseball." This was a believable story, but actually a myth. The authors then answer the question of who invented the game—actually, no one. Baseball evolved. The history of the game is traced from its pre-Revolutionary War status of a leisurely pastime to the billion-dollar industry it has become—thanks to the involvement of businessmen forming baseball teams and leagues and to a long line of amazing players like Ned Cuthbert (1863), who was the first to steal a base; Candy Cummings (1867), who invented the curve ball; and on to Cy Young, Ty Cobb, Lou Gehrig, Joe DiMaggio, Jackie Robinson, Roger Maris, and many more.

The economic, cultural, social, and political conditions of the country are woven into the history of the game. Filled with marvelous black-and-white photo reproductions, as well as quotes, the book is a very readable source for answers to many questions about the great American game.

Glossary: No
Bibliography: No
Index: Yes
Level: Intermediate New Readers

Watkins, David. *Camping and Walking.* Tulsa, OK: EDC, 1992.

Pages: 128
Series: An Usborne Guide

Anyone who enjoys camping and walking, is interested in these activities, or who needs to identify the necessary equipment and review the requirements for a successful adventure will find this guide completely satisfying. Concise, practical information covers every aspect of the subject: preparation and packing, clothing, finding and choosing a site, setting up camp, outdoor sleeping, cooking equipment, campfires and cooking, striking camp, appropriate walking gear, planning the route, exploring towns and the country-side, identifying land forms, understanding the weather, orienteering (with a test of map-reading and compass skills), and more. Other invaluable topics are hints for beginners, recipes, knot-tying, appropriate woods for campfires, map types, different cloud formations, finding direction by the stars, and compasses and how to use them. The combination of clear, simple language and captioned color and black-and-white illustrations results in a comprehensive reference source and take-along guide.

Glossary: No
Bibliography: No
Index: Yes
Level: Beginning–Intermediate New Readers

Wright, Gary. *Track and Field: A Step-by-Step Guide.* Mahwah, NJ: Troll, 1997.

Pages: 64
Series: Be the Best

Here is a brief summary of track and field history followed by short chapters on equipment, the layout of a track and field stadium, the required training (jogging, stretching, calisthenics, conditioning), sprints and dashes, middle-distance running, long-distance running, hurdles relays, and field events (long jump, high jump, javelin throw, discus throw, and shot-put). The appropriate technique for each event is explained and illustrated in black-and-white drawings. The brevity of the book, its simple language, the young people pictured, and the reference in the foreword to "boy and girl" identify this as a juvenile title. Nonetheless the adult beginning reader should find this step-by-step guide useful.

Glossary: No
Bibliography: No
Index: Yes
Level: Beginning New Readers

Transportation

Casanellas, Antonio. *Great Discoveries and Inventions That Improved Transportation.* Milwaukee, WI: Gareth Stevens, 2000.

Pages: 32
Series: Great Discoveries and Inventions

This brief text efficiently examines the evolution of land, sea, and air transportation, with a comparison of primitive early models and the ultramodern vehicles of today, including the first electric train in operation in 1879 compared with the high-speed trains of France, Germany, and Japan that float on the tracks; an 1885 motorcycle in contrast to a large-cylinder cycle of today; and ships of ancient Greece as opposed to a nuclear submarine.

There are illustrated fact boxes on related topics—how electric trains work, the mechanics of the motorcycle's two-stroke engine; ships of ancient Greece; the caravel used by Columbus and Magellan; how paddle steamers work; a look at a jet engine; the workings of a propeller; and how the hovercraft works. Many of the detailed illustrations are cutaways and serve to clarify the text.

There are eight projects on such topics as friction, the Archemedes Principle, and aerodynamic design, aimed at the juvenile reader, with perhaps some interest to adults motivated to try them out. This book will interest adults seeking basic information, particularly those with limited command of English.

Glossary: Yes
Bibliography: Yes, of books, videos, and Web sites

Index: Yes
Level: Beginning New Readers

Graham, Ian. *Spacecraft.* Illustrated by Roger Stewart. Orlando, FL: Raintree/Heinemann, 1995.

Pages: 32
Series: Pointers

A perfect source for adults looking for information about spacecraft, this book provides essential facts, that is, the craft's name, whether it was manned or unmanned, its dimensions, the names of those on board, the date it launched, purpose of its journey, and its landing. Full-color, detailed illustrations with numbered red pointers call attention to various features in the design of satellites, space capsules, shuttles, deep space probes, and space stations. Each pointer has a corresponding brief explanation (with the number printed in boldface).

Glossary: Yes
Bibliography: No
Index: Yes
Level: Beginning New Readers

Gunston, Bill. *The World of Flight.* Milwaukee, WI: Gareth Stevens, 2001.

Pages: 48
Series: An Inside Look

In 1873, the Montgolfier balloon, incredibly made from cloth and paper held together by over 2,000 buttons, was the first aircraft to carry people. Hot air balloons have come a long way since then, as has aviation in general. Two-page spreads with introductory paragraphs and captioned and labeled illustrations point out the features of each mode of flight—airships, the first airplane, early airplanes, how planes fly, the control mechanisms and surfaces, the cockpit, airplane parts, power systems, air traffic control, radar, helicopter flight, the Harrier warplane, and more. This book is a quick reference source for adults seeking a brief overview of the subject.

Glossary: Yes
Bibliography: Yes, of books, videos, and Web sites
Index: Yes
Level: Beginning New Readers

Herring, Peter. *Ultimate Train.* New York: DK, 2000.

Pages: 168
Series: —

This comprehensive book begins with a short history of trains from Watt's static engine to the first steam locomotive built by Cornish inventor Richard Trevithick, whose second (1804) steam engine did run, but its weight broke the rails. Enter George Stevenson and his Locomotion No. 1, the first steam engine to operate on a public rail-road. From this point on, the British railroad system grew and jumped across the Atlantic where, by 1869, one could travel from New York to San Francisco by rail. This historical overview then traces the development of rail systems from steam to diesel, to electric, to maglevs (magnetic levitation systems).

The second section, "Ultimate Trains," highlights the designs of locomotives during the periods 1800–1840, 1840–1870, 1870–1900, 1900–1920, 1920–1940, 1940–1970, and 1970–2000, ending with a glimpse into the future. The third section, which includes black-and-white photographs, lists railroad innovators alphabetically by name and provides a short description of their lives and achievements.

Typical of DK style, each two-page spread has an introductory paragraph, lush captioned color photographs with parts labeled, and some cutaways. Highlighted boxes contain the specifications of some significant locomotives in history. This rich, comprehensive look at trains is an excellent reference volume, as well as a coffee table treat for both adults and children.

Glossary: Yes, including a chart of common steam locomotive types
Bibliography: No

Index: Yes, with numbers in italic indicating illustrations
Level: Beginning–Advanced New Readers

Humble, Richard. *Ships: Sailors and the Sea.* New York: Franklin Watts, 1991.

Pages: 48
Series: Timelines

Rich with remarkable pictures, maps, and cutaways to show the internal structures of various types of vessels, this book sails the reader through a comprehensive overview of the history of ships. Included are the earliest boats built by the ancient Egyptians, Greek and Roman oared war galleys, Viking war and trading longships, European full-rigged sailing ships (with foremast, mainmast, and mizzenmast), Arab dhows, Portugese caravels used by Columbus, great English battleships built during the reign of Henry VIII, galleons of the Spanish Armada, seventeenth- and eighteenth-century European war and cargo ships, nineteenth-century steamships, modern battleships and submarines, and twentieth-century luxury liners, aircraft carriers, guided-missile warships, sporting craft, speedy hydrofoils and hovercraft ferries, luxury yachts, oil tankers, and future computer-controlled, solar-powered ships. An illustrated chronology provides a snapshot view of the development of ships for war and peace and lists some famous vessels, seamen, voyages, and battles. This book is a fine source of quick information about maritime history.

Glossary: Yes, of selected terms not clearly defined in the text
Bibliography: No
Index: Yes, with reference to illustrations in boldface
Level: Beginning–Intermediate New Readers

Jefferis, David. *Aircraft.* New York: DK, 2004.

Pages: 128
Series: Pocket Guides

An introductory section discusses how aircraft are used and provides a glimpse of the first attempts at flight, first flights, and early aviators. Subsequent sections examine the inside of an aircraft, airliners from prop planes to supersonic aircraft, light aircraft, seaplanes and amphibians, combat aircraft, air battles, dog fights and bomber raids, vertical takeoff, helicopter and jet lift, navigation and safety equipment, and the "leading edge"—from X planes to electronic and computerized systems and on to future aircraft.

Just about everything one needs to know about aircraft is packed into this little book. Each section begins with a brief introductory text and excellent full-color photos with informative captions. A time line of aircraft, an illustrated list of inventors and pioneers of aircraft development, a two-page list of aviation heroes, and amazing aircraft facts are included. The book is a handy quick-reference guide.

Glossary: Yes
Bibliography: No, but a list of resources, museums, and air displays
Index: Yes
Level: Intermediate New Reader

Johnstone, Michael, Chris Grigg, and Keith Harmer. *Trains.*
New York: Scholastic, 2001.

Pages: 32
Series: Look Inside Cross-Sections

Any train buff should find this brief look at the evolution of locomotive design attractive. Of course, there are many different models world-wide, but the aim of this book is to provide a close-up view of the anatomy of the locomotives that represent milestones in history. "Little Rocket," which debuted in Liverpool in 1829, proved that the steam locomotives were a practical mode of transportation. The 1849 Crampton No. 122 completed the first express trip from Paris to Calais. Other notable trains are mentioned: the American 4-4-0, the workhorse of early American railroads of the 1800s; the 1870 English Stirling "Single," noted for its huge eight-foot driving wheels that allowed it to achieve high speeds; the early-twentieth-century tank engine, built for short runs, which carried its water and coal supplies on the engine; the 4-12-2 very large class of steam locomotive, introduced in 1926 by the Union Pacific Railroad, designed to haul freight and passengers long distances; the speedy Pacific class engine, built by the Missouri Pacific Railroad in 1902 and in England in 1922; the rack locomotive, patented by the Swiss railroad engineer Roman Abt, designed to push or pull trains up steep hills using a rack and pinion system; the class 73 electrodiesel engine, which began its run on the British Railway system in 1962; and the 1994 Le Shuttle, which runs through the English Channel Tunnel between Folkestone, England, and Calais, France.

Each chapter has a brief introductory text with a picture of the outside of the locomotive. The full two-page illustrations that slice through various sections of the locomotives to reveal the working parts are clearly labeled and surrounded by brief facts about designers, historical dates and events, and operational techniques and definitions of specific features. Highlighted boxes contain line drawings of the models and important technical data. A pictorial time line neatly summarizes the text.

Glossary: Yes, with illustrations for some of the terms
Bibliography: No
Index: Yes
Level: Beginning–Itermediate New Reader

Kroll, Steven. *Pony Express!* New York: Scholastic, 2000.

Pages: 40
Series: —

The attractive format of this book and its exciting, well-written text capture the spirit and drama of the Pony Express. This mail delivery service ran between Saint Joseph, Missouri, and Sacramento, California, for a grueling 18 months in the 1860s in an effort to speed up mail delivery service between the east and west coasts via an overland route. Each page of text is accompanied by wood-grain framed oil paintings showing the Pony Express riders in action. A map of the Pony Express route and photographs that illustrate major events in the development of the modern postal service are useful additions to the book. It is an excellent brief history for anyone interested in this fascinating period of mail delivery service.

Glossary: No
Bibliography: Yes
Index: Yes
Level: Beginning–Intermediate New Readers

Loves, June. *Ships.* Broomall, PA: Chelsea House, 2001.

Pages: 32
Series: Database Transportation

A short introduction clarifies the difference between ships and boats—a source of confusion for many who use the terms interchangeably. A four-page history of ships looks at the first boats, those of ancient Egyptians and Phonecians, sailing ships, famous explorers, clippers, steam ships, paddle steamers, packets, and passenger liners, the Titanic in particular. Kinds of ships, from the smallest to the largest, from canoes to cargo and naval ships, are briefly defined. A double-page cutaway shows the various parts of a passenger ship. Following pages explain and illustrate parts of ships and boats and how they navigate. There is a brief look at future designs of vessels.

Brief text and ample color illustrations are presented in a computer database format that aims to provide a lesson in computer literacy as one navigates the book. Those looking for brief facts on the subject, including people with a limited command of English, will find this book helpful

Glossary: Yes
Bibliography: No
Index: Yes
Level: Beginning New Readers

Mander, Lelia. *Start the Car.* Farmington Hills, MI: Thomson Gale, 2004.

Pages: 48
Series: Step Back Science

This book contains facts that every driver should know. It opens with a simple combination of text, captioned illustrations, and a diagram of a car showing where, under the hood, the engine, battery, fuel tank, accelerator, and ignition are. Then the reader finds out how the key makes the car start, where the electric current comes from, what, other than the battery, makes the car run, the function of the spark plugs, engine timing, where the gas comes from, grades of gas, how gas is refined, and what the origin of crude oil is and what it is made of. There is a double-page spread of car facts and figures, including a time line of inventions who contributed to the development of the car. A page of three questions and answers is included.

This is a short and sweet explication of basic information. It is ideal for adults who have no clue about the inner workings of a car.

Glossary: Yes
Bibliography: Yes
Index: Yes
Level: Beginning New Readers

Nahum, Andrew. *Flying Machine.* New York: DK, 2004.

Pages: 72
Series: Eyewitness

This excellent guide to aircraft is packed with information on the history of flight. It covers many types of aircraft from kites (flown in China over 3,000 years ago) to gliders, the Wright brothers' gasoline-powered flying machine, and on to single-engine planes, the first passenger aircraft (the 1933 Boeing 247) to the modern-day jet liner. The book is rich with details on the principle of flight, the inner workings of various planes, the clothing the first pilots wore, how wings provide lift, facts about airplane engines, propellers, an inside-out look at a jetliner, an explanation of jet propulsion, a look at the landing gear, the cockpit, the flying instruments, how a helicopter works—in short, a close-up view of all aspects of flight.

The book includes a double-page spread on amazing facts, questions and answers, and a list of airplane record breakers. A who's who section provides brief biographical information on pioneers of flight, inventors, engineers and designers, manufacturers, and aviators. Marvelous captioned and labeled color photographs illuminate the book.

Glossary: Yes
Bibliography: No, but a list of museums and Web sites to visit
Index: Yes
Level: Beginning–Intermediate New Readers

Sandler, Martin W. *Straphanging in the U.S.A.: Trolleys and Subways in American Life.* New York: Oxford University Press, 2003.

Pages: 64
Series: Transportation in America

The first horse-drawn omnibus line in the United States, as well as the first urban public transportation system, came on the scene in 1831 in New York City and became so popular that they multiplied rapidly in New York, Boston, Philadelphia, and Baltimore. Because of the resulting chaos from congested streets, new, more efficient modes of rapid transit soon followed: the elevated train, subway system, cable railway, trolley line, interurban line, monorail, San Francisco's BART (Bay Area Rapid Transit), and light rail systems. Sandler provides details on the technological innovations that made these forms of transportation possible. The effects of these rail systems on American life are discussed. Mass transportation was inexpensive and efficient, electricity was pollution free, rails reduced congestion on city streets, and they stretched out to the country, creating suburbs.

Embellished with numerous archival photographs, drawings, illustrations and quotes from magazines, newspapers, and books, the book is a fascinating read. Highlighted pages provide related information on the sizes and shapes of horse cars, buses for cities and schools, and cheers for the nation's first subway. A time line is included. This title is a good choice for both researchers and casual readers with an interest in the subject.

Glossary: No
Bibliography: Yes, of books and addresses, telephone numbers, and
     Web sites of transit museums
Index: Yes
Level: Beginning–Advanced New Readers

Steins, Richard. *Transportation Milestones and Breakthroughs.* Austin, TX: Steck-Vaughn, 1996.

Pages: 48
Series: Twenty Events

A short introduction to inventions, people, and events that profoundly affected the evolution of transportation, this book consists of 20 topics covered on facing pages. A very readable descriptive text is well illustrated with photographs, charts, maps, etc. The topics include the wheel, the Appian Way, the Conestoga wagon, the bicycle, clipper ships, the Otis elevator, the London underground, "Kon Tiki," Vostok I, and the Concorde. This title is appropriate for those looking for quick facts, dates, and historical summaries.

Glossary: Yes
Bibliography: Yes
Index: Yes, with references to the 20 topics in boldface
Level: Beginning New Readers

Sutton, Richard and Laura Butler. *Car.* New York: DK, 2005.

Pages: 72
Series: Eyewitness

This is the perfect book for the person who wants to learn about the history of the automobile and to understand the mechanics of cars. Readers will no doubt be interested to discover that the first car to be sold to the public (in 1885) came out of the Karl Benz workshop in Mannheim, Germany. But this mode of transportation was reserved for the rich until Henry Ford built his Model T, using a production line to build more cars faster so that they could be sold for less to more people. The book shows how automobile styles changed over the years and describes the anatomy of a car and how the various components (spark plugs, drive train, steering, brakes, etc.) evolved and operate. Each two-page section begins with a brief introductory paragraph. Captions to the clearly labeled pictures and cutaway photographs make comprehension quite easy.

Glossary: No
Bibliography: No
Index: Yes, excellent
Level: Beginning–Intermediate New Readers

Weitzman, David. *A Subway for New York.* New York: Farrar, Straus, Giroux, 2005.

Pages: 40
Series: —

In 1863, London opened the world's first subway system—followed by subways in Budapest and Glasgow in 1896, Paris in 1900, Berlin in 1902, and, across the Atlantic, in Boston in 1898. New York soon followed and started the huge construction job on February 21, 1900, when Contract No. 1 was signed to build the IRT (Interborough Rapid Transit) that would initially run from the northern end of Manhattan to its southern tip, following under Broadway and terminating at City Hall. Weitzman presents a close-up view of this massive undertaking in words and detailed black-and-white illustrations of the stages of construction, as well as the richly designed stations and kiosks. On October 4, 1904, the first section opened to carry passengers from City Hall to 145th Street and Broadway. This experience in rapid transit cost a modest nickel. Today the subway has 722 miles of track along 244 miles of routes and carries over 1 billion riders a year who pay a much higher fare than the initial five cents. This look under the New York City sidewalks is a captivating read for adults—particularly train buffs.

Glossary: No
Bibliography: No, but has a paragraph on suggested further readings
Index: No
Level: Beginning–Intermediate New Readers

Wilkinson, Philip. *The World of Ships*. Boston: Kingfisher, 2005.

Pages: 64
Series: —

Wilkinson's examination of the world of ships is divided into four sections: "Trade and Discovery," "Ships of War," "Peopling the World," and "Discovering Ships." Each section focuses on a variety of subjects. "Trade and Discovery" looks at early traders, such as Magellan, DaGama, Cabot, and Barents, and a double-page map traces their routes with color-coded lines and arrows. A pictorial view of trading ships shows different types, from the ancient Egyptian small sailing boat to the modern container vessel. Following are nine double-page spreads with close-up views of various trading ships, from the earliest to today's modern cargo ships. A two-page spread on piracy is appropriately illustrated with a black background.

"Ships of War" opens with a double-page feast of quick information against a background of a map on a radar screen. There is a two-column list of memorable battles, from Salamis in 480 BC to Midway in 1942. Types of battleships are identified in words and pictures at the bottom of the page. Following are six double-page spreads giving further information on types of warships.

"Peopling the World" opens with a double-page map of the world with boxed facts on the California gold rush, Viking settlers, 1800s migration to the United States and Canada, slave trade, refugees from Vietnam, and more. These topics are further discussed in five double-page spreads. There is a cross-section view of the galleon *Mayflower*, the SS *Great Britain*, and the luxury liner *Grand Princess*.

"Discovering Ships," the final section, evaluates the roles of ships, shipbuilding, navigation technologies, and researchers. Again, a world map dominates the opening double-page spread. Boxes contain facts about particular vessels, and red lines point to their locations on the map, for example, the *Exxon Valdez*, the US *Constitution*, the *Vasa*, and the *Titanic*, as well as ships from the Orient, built by the Vikings, and in the Spanish Armada. Additional double-page spreads look at myths and mysteries of the sea, other kinds of vessels (e.g., factory ships, salvage vessels, and catamarans), and shipwrecks.

This attractive title is a quick reference source. It is also ideal for browsing.

Glossary: Yes
Bibliography: No
Index: Yes
Level: Beginning–Intermediate New Readers

Wilkinson, Philip and Michael Pollard. *Transportation.*
Illustrated by Robert Ingpen. New York: Chelsea House, 1995.

Pages: 93
Series: Ideas That Changed the World

This comprehensive pictorial history of the evolution of transportation begins thousands of years ago with the invention of the wheel, which was reinvented in the nineteenth century as an air-filled leather tire (by Robert Thomson [1822–1873]) and then as an air-filled tube encased in rubber (John Boyd Dunlop [1840–1921]). The authors trace the development of roads, boats and ships, navigational devices (compasses and chronometers), steam engines, internal combustion engines, the automobile, aircraft, propeller and jet engines, and rockets and space travel. Captioned pictures show what the various inventions looked like at different stages of development, as well as how some of the devices operate. Some famous inventors are also introduced. Many pages contain highlighted boxes with interesting supplementary information, such as facts about the fastest and largest sailing ships, opposition to the use of steam locomotives, the invention of the bicycle, and space litter.

Glossary: No
Bibliography: Yes
Index: Yes
Level: Intermediate New Readers

Woods, Michael and Mary B. Woods. *Ancient Transportation: From Camels to Canals.* Minneapolis: Runestone Press, 2000.

Pages: 96
Series: Ancient Technology

This survey of transportation technology in various cultures from the Stone Age to AD 476, including ancient Middle East, India, China, Egypt, Mesoamerica, Greece, and Rome, is concise and easy to read. Fascinating information on such early modes of transportation as dugout canoes, skis and sledges, rafts, floats, junks, freighters, and more is presented. The authors point out that moving quickly and carrying heavy loads from one place to another was vital to survival. The first bridges were formed naturally by fallen trees, and the first bridge builder was the first person to fell a tree or move a log to cross a river or ravine. The first boats were floating objects, followed by rafts, dugout canoes, and bark boats. Related topics such as roads, maps, wheels and axles, canals (the first Suez Canal was built in the thirteenth century BC), compasses, lighthouses, bridges and ports are discussed.

A map of the civilizations of the ancient world through AD 476, sidebars, and clear photos of artifacts enhance the book. A fascinating, easy-to-read primary source on the origins of transportation technology, this title provides the adult reader with a concise overview of the subject in just seven fact-filled chapters.

Glossary: Yes
Bibliography: Yes
Index: Yes
Level: Beginning–Intermediate New Readers

Yepsen, Roger B. *City Trains: Moving Through America's Cities by Rail.* Macmillan, 1993.

Pages: 96
Series: —

Horse cars (street cars using horse power), streetcars, cable cars, subways, elevated trains, inclined railways, interurban railways, commuter trains, and monorails; high-speed maglev (magnetic levitation); the growth of cities as centers of business, industry, culture, and art; and population expansion to the suburbs are covered in this well-illustrated overview of the development of urban rail systems. The operating principles of the various types of train are easily grasped—for example, the operation of a cable car is likened to a clothesline of wash looped on pulleys. Developing and utilizing new types of trains while considering environmental health and the future of cities is emphasized throughout. The combination of a very readable text and interesting black-and-white photographs makes this an excellent first source and introduction to more advanced material.

Glossary: No
Bibliography: Yes, of books, magazines, videos, and the names of
    rail museums
Index: Yes
Level: Intermediate–Advanced New Readers

❋ Bibliography of Professional ❋ Resources Consulted

Benham, Frances and Ronald R. Powell. *Success in Answering Reference Questions: Two Studies.* Metuchen, NJ: Scarecrow Press, 1987.

Brundin, Robert E. "The Place of the Practicum in Teaching Reference Interview Techniques." *The Reference Librarian* 25/26 (1989): 449–464.

Bundy, Mary L., M. Bridgman, and Laura Keltie. "Public Library Reference Service: Myth and Reality." *Public Library Quarterly* 3(3) (1982): 11–22.

Bunge, Charles A. "Interpersonal Dimensions of the Reference Interview: A Historical Review." *Drexel Library Quarterly* (Spring 1984): 4–23.

Crowley, Terence and Thomas Childers. *Information Service in Public Libraries: Two Studies.* Metuchen, NJ: Scarecrow Press, 1971.

Farrelly, Michael Garrett. "Bother the Librarians!" *Public Libraries* 46(1) (January/February 2007): 36–38.

Hauptman, Robert. "The Myth of the Reference Interview." *The Reference Librarian* 16 (Winter 1986): 47–52.

Heiser, Jane C. "Libraries, Literacy and Lifelong Learning: The Reference Connection." *The Reference Librarian* 16 (Winter 1986): 109–124.

Hosskisson, T. "Making the Right Assumptions: Know Your User and Improve the Reference Interview." *The Reference Librarian* 28 (1997): 67–75.

Jahoda, Gerald. "Rules for Performing Steps in the Reference Process." *The Reference Librarian* 25/26 (1989): 557–567.

Katz, Bill and Ruth A. Fraley, eds. *Evolution of Reference Services*, vol. II, *The Reference Librarian.* Binghamton, NY: The Haworth Press, 1984.

Katz, William A. "Basic Information Sources." vol. 1, in *Introduction to Reference Work*, 8th ed. New York: McGraw-Hill, 2002: 15–21.

Kern, Kathleen. "Communication, Patron Satisfaction, and the Reference Interview." *Reference & User Services Quarterly* 43(1) (Fall 2003): 47–49.

Kuruppu, Pali U. "Evaluation of Reference Services—A Review." *Journal of Academic Librarianship* 33(3) (May 2007): 368–381.

Lynch, Mary Jo. "Reference Interviews in Public Libraries." *Library Quarterly* 48 (April 1978): 119–142.

Mabry, C.H. "The Reference Interview as Partnership: An Examination of Librarian, Library User and Social Interaction." *The Reference Librarian* 40 (1983–1984): 41–56.

Murphy, Sarah Anne. "The Reference Narrative." *Reference & User Services Quarterly* 44(3) (Spring 2005): 247–252.

Oser, Fred. "Reference Simplex or the Mysteries of Reference Interviewing Revealed." *The Reference Librarian* 16 (Winter 1986): 53–78.

Radford, Marie. "Communication Theory Applied to the Reference Encounter." *Library Quarterly* 66(2) (April 1996): 123–137.

Rosow, LaVergne. *Light and Lively Reads for ESL, Adult and Teen Readers.* Englewood, CO: Libraries Unlimited, 1996.

Ross, C.J. "The Reference Interview: Why It Needs to Be Used in Every (Well Almost Every) Reference Transaction." *Reference & User Services Quarterly* 43(1) (Fall 2003): 38–43.

Ross, Catherine Sheldrick and Patricia Dewdney. "Negative Closure: Strategies and Counter Strategies in the Reference Transaction." *Reference & User Services Quarterly* 38(2) (1998): 151–163.

Selnick, Shari. "READ/Orange County: Changing Lives Through Literacy." Public Libraries 43(1) (January/February 2004): 53–56.

Stephens, Annabel K. "Twenty-First Century Public Library Adult Services." *Reference & User Services Quarterly* 45(3) (Spring 2006): 223–235.

Taylor, Robert. "Question Negotiation and Information Seeking in Libraries." *College & Research Libraries* 29 (May 1968): 178–184.

Tycoson, David. "Reference at its Core: The Reference Interview." *Reference & User Services Quarterly* 43(1) (Fall 2003): 49–51.

Tycoson, David A. "Wrong Questions: Wrong Answers: Behavioral vs. Factual Valuation of Reference Service." *The Reference Librarian* 38 (1992): 151–173.

Weibel, Marguerite Crowley. *Choosing and Using Books with Adult New Readers.* New York: Neal-Schuman, 1996.

Westbrook, Lynn. "Virtual Reference Training: The Second Generation." *College & Research Libraries* 67(3) (May 2006): 249–259.

White, Marilyn Domas. "Different Approaches to the Reference Interview." *The Reference Librarian* 25/26 (1989): 641–646.

❧ Author Index ❧

�֍ Title Index �֍

�֎ Series Index �֎

✖ Subject Index ✖

✖ About the Author ✖

Rosemarie Riechel is a writer and researcher and a member of the American Library Association, The Society of Children's Book Writers and Illustrators, and the Long Island Society of Children's Writers and Illustrators. She has a Master of Library Science, an Advanced Certificate Degree, and a Doctor of Library Science from Columbia University. As head of the Information, Public Catalog and Telephone Reference Division of the Queens Borough Public Library in New York for a number of years, Dr. Riechel was responsible also for policies, procedures, and staff training for online systems and services. She is the author of a number of books on library science, including *Public Library Services to Business, Reference Services for Children and Young Adults,* and *Improving Telephone Information and Reference Service in Public Libraries.* She has also published articles on public library reference service and online searching in periodicals and proceedings. Dr. Riechel is the librarian for the Long Island Parrot Society, Babylon, New York, and contributes a column to the monthly newsletter. A children's book, *Flight to Freedom: Two Parrot Stories,* was published in 2007.